■SCHOLASTIC

Teaching Effective Classroom Routines

Establish Structure in the Classroom to Foster Children's Learning— From the First Day of School and All Through the Year

by Deborah Diffily and Charlotte Sassman

NEW YORK • TORONTO • LONDON • AUCKLAND • SYDNEY
MEXICO CITY • NEW DELHI • HONG KONG • BUENOS AIRES

Teaching *Resources*

ACKNOWLEDGMENT

Our work in early childhood classrooms is the guiding force for this book. Looking in the eyes of real children is the best reality check there is. The children who are, and have been, in our classes are the real authors of this book. They have shaped it—and our teaching.

Over the years, we've learned to look at changing children's behavior as a process, something we support rather than something we control. We see classroom discipline as an opportunity to teach children important life skills. We've learned to celebrate the small accomplishments of young children, especially when it comes to changing their behaviors. We recall dozens of stories when thinking about appreciating small changes in behavior, but this one always makes us smile. When Major, a smiling, active, five-year-old, came to school, he was used to doing and saying whatever he pleased. His parental support was spotty—his grandmother attempted to "keep him in line"—but when he stayed with his mother, he heard and saw things far beyond his years. When Major was frustrated or angry, he expressed his distaste with words that would embarrass the most salty sailor. His teacher, the principal, and other teachers worked with Major to help him learn to control his choice of vocabulary. One day the principal stopped by his classroom to check on him. She asked him, "Major, how are you doing with your words today?" With a smile that would dazzle anyone, he proudly stated, "I'm doing good! I did not say 'f——' once today!" She sighed and, once again, talked to him about choosing his words carefully. Major was making progress—although he still had a long way to go—and the adults at school wisely kept supporting him until they did not have to have these conversations with him anymore.

Conversations with Maria L. Chang, our editor at Scholastic Teaching Resources, and Liza Charlesworth started our thoughts about how to record what we do in guiding young children's behavior. Thanks to both of you. We also appreciate Beth Saladino and Sherri Coughey for reading our first draft and making comments that directed our revisions.

Finally, we acknowledge our colleagues and their influence on our views about guiding children's behavior. The ongoing dialogue, study groups, and research about how to best support young children have been invaluable. And, as always, we appreciate the sage ways of young children everywhere.

Cover design by James Sarfati
Cover photographs by Jon Freilich/Getty Images
Interior design by Holly Grundon

ISBN 0-439-51380-4
Copyright © 2004 by Deborah Diffily and Charlotte Sassman
All rights reserved. Published by Scholastic Inc.
Printed in the U.S.A.

3 4 5 6 7 8 9 10   40   10 09 08 07 06 05 04

Contents

Introduction

A successful school year for young children and their teachers depends on several factors. Curriculum is important. Learning materials are important. Lesson plans are important. But perhaps the most important factor in the success of a school year is the issue of guidance—or classroom management or discipline. It does not matter which term you use to describe what teachers do to get children to act in certain ways, but it is critically important to know how to support children as they learn how to behave in ways that are appropriate for school.

Equally important to the issue of guidance is the establishment of classroom routines. When routines are clearly in place, the class operates much more smoothly. They make the way children learn to work together much better. Teachers need to set up procedures for everything that they want students to do. When the expectations for behaviors are clearly explained to children and routines are practiced, the class simply operates more effectively and efficiently.

The ways that children behave in the classroom affect all of the activities that go on in that room. If viewed only from the perspective of the amount of time that the teacher spends teaching versus the amount of time that he or she spends correcting children's behavior, it is obviously much better to have students who do what they are expected to do. If viewed from the perspective of what children can learn from each other when they are cooperating versus when they are arguing, it is clearly better to have students who get along with each other. If viewed from the perspective of children learning the social skills they need as successful students and successful adults versus simply preventing arguments, it is obviously better to have students who have developed competent social skills. Classes run more smoothly when children are considerate, cooperative, and socially competent.

> Teachers have long known and researchers are now confirming that social skills are not just something to be taught to children so that they behave well enough to get on with the real business of schooling. Rather, they are inextricably intertwined with cognitive growth and intellectual growth.
> —Roxann Kriete, 1999

The question then becomes, what can teachers do to help students develop these characteristics? We believe that students become more considerate when they are involved in creating the rules and routines that guide their behaviors at school than when they are taught to follow prescribed rules. We think they become more cooperative when they analyze their behavior against the rules and routines they helped establish than when the teacher dictates punishment for breaking the rules. We know that children treat each other more respectfully and become more socially competent when they are asked to think about other people's feelings than when these issues are ignored at school.

Beyond the characteristics related to social development, we believe that being an integral part of deciding how the class will operate positively affects children's cognitive development. Children develop higher-order thinking skills, such as analysis and evaluation, when they think about the different kinds of behavior that are required at school. We believe that children learn much more when they are active in the process of establishing rules and routines than when they simply conform to teacher-created rules.

Managing vs. Guiding Children's Behavior

Virtually everyone agrees that children need to learn the behavior that is expected of them in the classroom and in school. There are many ways to go about this, but most of these ways fall into two basic categories. One is by managing children's behavior. The other is by guiding children's behavior.

More children change their behaviors—over time—when their teachers help them understand how their behavior affects others.

When adults manage children's behavior, the rules and the teacher are dominant. The focus of classroom management is to get children to act in appropriate ways whether they understand the reasons for the rules or not. In classes where the teacher believes in managing behavior, it is always the teacher who sets up the rules, usually before even meeting students. The teacher also determines what the consequences will be for breaking the rules. Typically, the consequences are general ones—sitting in time-out, missing portions of recess, having a note sent home, calling parents from school, and so on. The consequence is not necessarily related to the specific rule that was breached. And it is the teacher who judges when a rule has been broken and metes out punishment to the offending student(s).

When adults guide children's behavior, they view getting children to act in appropriate ways differently. They begin by recognizing that children are in the process of learning acceptable behavior. They see inappropriate behavior as an opportunity to teach children, not as a situation where that behavior must be stopped immediately.

For example, a typical rule in early childhood classes is "Keep hands, feet, and objects to yourself." In a class where the teacher manages student behavior and rules are dominant, the teacher would punish the child who pushed into a group of children at the beginning of story

time. Obviously, this child had put her hands and feet on other children and broken an established rule. Depending on the list of consequences used in that class, the teacher might write the child's name on the board, make the child pull her green card, or announce that the child would miss five minutes of recess. In a class where the teacher guides children's behavior and views

I wanted them to do the right thing because it was the right thing to do, not because they were going to get something.

inappropriate behavior as a teaching opportunity, the teacher would react differently. The teacher would ask the children who had been pushed or stepped on to tell the offending child how they felt about what had happened. The teacher might ask the class what the child could have done differently so other people did not get hurt. If no suggestions were forthcoming from the class, the teacher might make a suggestion of her own, asking that child to try these words, "Could you please move over a little bit so I can sit beside you?"

There is a big difference between how that child—and other children in the class—would feel in the first teacher's class as opposed to the second teacher's class. Many children in classes where punishment reigns do change their behaviors, but the motivating factor is to "stay out of trouble." Some children do not care about punishment, so their behaviors rarely change in classrooms where the teacher tries to control children. More children change their behaviors—over time—when their teachers help them understand how their behavior affects others.

Comments
From a Kindergarten Teacher

I've been teaching kindergarten for ten years now. In my college classes professors always emphasized how important it was to set up rules on the first day of school and be consistent in enforcing every single rule, every time one was broken. When I started teaching, I heard the same thing from experienced teachers and from principals: Establish the rules and enforce them.

A couple of years into my teaching career, I began hearing about how unfair it was to only punish children who broke rules. Now, we were supposed to reward those children who were following the rules, so as I posted class rules and consequences of breaking the rules, I also posted a list of what happened when children followed the rules. Like all the other teachers in my school, I began handing out candies as a reward for following directions, dropping marbles into a jar when the whole class did something well and having popcorn parties when the jar was full, maintaining sticker charts for individual children's good behavior, and handing out school bucks for following the rules and taking children to the school store every Friday afternoon so they could "buy" treats with their earned bucks. All of those things seemed to grow over the years. The last year I did all of those things, I began feeling like managing my students' behavior was taking up more of my time than actually teaching. It also seemed like children needed more candy to keep them on task and students would ask for a sticker, a school buck, or a marble for every little thing that they did.

At that point in my teaching career, I began looking for a better way to work with children. I wanted them to do the right thing because it was the right thing to do, not because they were going to get something. I wanted to spend more of my time teaching my students than manipulating their behavior. I started talking to teachers from other schools and reading journal articles and books that those teachers recommended. That's when

Comments (continued)

I made the decision to move away from management of children's behavior into guiding their behavior.

Gone are the punishments and rewards. Instead I look at children's behavior—especially their misbehavior—as teaching opportunities. Now my primary goal is to support the development of children's self-control instead of working toward students' compliance with the rules that I established. Basically, I've changed my whole way of thinking about student behavior. There is a tremendous difference in the atmosphere in my class, how children treat each other, and, I really think, how much my students learn.

This book offers specific suggestions for early childhood educators who want to guide children's behaviors. The suggestions are organized by what adults can do before the school year begins, and what they can do the first day, first week, and first month of school, as well as what can be done on a continuing basis throughout the year. Having worked with young children in establishing their own rules and routines for more than a decade, we are convinced that this is a better way to interact with and to teach children.

CHAPTER 1

BEFORE THE FIRST DAY:

Planning for Your Best Year Ever

Thinking about the first day of school generates feelings of both excitement and apprehension in most teachers. The excitement comes from the opportunity of a new school year to start fresh, to create a new community of learners, and to make a difference in the lives of children. The apprehension comes from the unknown. You may have dozens of questions, such as: What will my students be like? How many different learning styles will they have? How wide will the range of their abilities be? Will my students be well behaved? Will they get along? Will there be major personality conflicts?

> Teachers create a structure in which children experience a sense of belonging and know that they are valued members of the classroom community. The sense of order is not based on power, but on shared understandings.
>
> *— Toni S. Bickart,*
> *Judy R. Jablon, and*
> *Diane Trister Dodge, 1999*

You may not have the answers to these questions before school begins and until you have time to get to know your students. But there are some things you can do to support children's best behavior and their ability to get along with each other. Class rules and routines definitely affect children's behavior. Since these need to be explained during the first week of school, you should consider rules and routines and make decisions about these before the first day of school. The way you arrange the furniture in the classroom affects children's behavior. The way you organize supplies and materials affects children's behavior. Anticipating and taking care of these issues before children arrive in the classroom can make the school year run smoothly.

Making Decisions About Rules or Guidelines

Even before the school year begins, it is a good idea to spend some time thinking about how to develop and foster consideration, cooperation, and social competence in children. Part of this quest is to consider the class rules or guidelines you want to establish for your class, as well as plan for classroom routines. There are many questions related to these issues that require serious consideration. Some of these issues are:

> Routines establish a sense of order and stability. Life is easier for everyone when there is a smooth rhythm to events in the day.
> — Jane Nelsen, Lynn Lott, and H. Stephen Glenn, 2000

- Do I want to establish rules and explain them to children, or do I want to involve children in setting rules?

- Do I want to get away from hard and fast rules and introduce the idea of guidelines or class norms instead?

- Will I set up firm consequences that will apply to each and every child, or will I take into consideration different factors when deciding about consequences?

- Will I use rewards and punishments related to good and bad behavior, or is there a better way to help children learn behavior that is appropriate for school?

After you've decided on these issues, you still need to make decisions relating to routines:

- ◆ How will I get children to follow the class's routines?

- ◆ Should I involve the children in establishing the routines?

- ◆ Will chaos result if we have too many routines?

- ◆ What can children do on their own?

In making these decisions, it is helpful to consider what experts in the fields of education and psychology have written:

Behavior problems provide an excellent opportunity for both teachers and students to learn and practice life skills, such as showing concern for others and brainstorming to find solutions that are helpful to individuals and to the whole group. (Nelsen, Lott, and Glenn, 2000, p. 5)

Punishment is based on several false premises:

1. *To make children do better, first we have to make them feel worse.*

2. *It is more important to make children pay for what they have done than to learn from what they have done.*

3. *Children learn better through control and intimidation than through exploring the results of their choices in a nurturing environment.*

Would any of these methods inspire you to improve your behavior?
(Nelsen, Lott, and Glenn, 2000, p. 117)

. . . classroom management programs that rely on rewards and consequences ought to be avoided by any educator who wants students to take responsibility for their own (and others') behavior—and by any educator who places internalization of positive values ahead of mindless obedience.
(Kohn, 1994, p. 2)

This is one of the most thoroughly replicated findings in the field of social psychology: The more you reward people for doing something, the more they tend to lose interest in whatever they had to do to get the reward.
(Kohn, 1999, p. 98)

We need to approach the issues of classroom management and discipline as much more than what to do when children break rules and misbehave. Rather than simply reacting to problems, we need to establish an ongoing curriculum in self-control, social participation, and human development. We need to accept the potential of children to learn these things, and the potential of teachers to teach them. (Charney, 1991, p. 9)

We need to strive for the creation of self-control in children. It is the first purpose of classroom management. (Charney, 1991, p. 11)

The ideal aim of education is creation of power of self-control. (Dewey, 1938, p. 64)

There are two basic schools of thought about supporting children's behavior in the classroom. Some teachers favor rules. Generally they think children need specific regulations with defined punishment for misbehavior. The punishment remains the same no matter what misbehavior the child does. That is, if you break any rule, you are punished according to the established system. Other teachers prefer guidelines that children help create. They offer multiple opportunities for children to internalize these guidelines, modifying them as needed. Consequences are tied to the guideline rather than a unilaterally enforced punishment. We believe that working with children to establish guidelines is the best way to prepare them to live independent lives.

Establishing Rules

Early childhood educators, like teachers everywhere, have a choice about how they communicate their expectations for behavior in the classroom. Some teachers choose to share rules that they create, posting them on the first day of school and explaining them to children.

If you decide to set rules and introduce them to children, it is important that all children understand each rule. Obviously you'll explain each rule, but it is important for young children to go beyond verbal explanations. Good teachers involve children in discussions about rules, role-playing what it looks like to follow each rule, and perhaps even drawing pictures of themselves following the rules. If there are consequences for breaking a class rule, it is critically important that teachers ensure that all children understand each rule and each consequence.

If you decide to involve students in creating class rules, this takes more time. First, introduce the idea of class rules as being important for keeping all students safe and for reminding everyone how to treat each other. Then guide several conversations about class rules, often leading the discussion with direct questions, such as "Do you think we need to have a class rule about how we talk to each other? How do you want other people to talk to you? Is it okay for us to use a mean voice when we talk to each other, or do we want people to speak respectfully to us?" As rules are developed and the class agrees on the wording of each rule, you and your students need to discuss consequences for breaking each rule. Teachers who believe children should create their own rules typically believe that consequences for breaking those rules ought to be logical, related to the specific rule. For example, if the rule "Keep hands, feet, and objects to yourself" is broken during a whole-group learning experience, then the consequence might be to sit slightly separated from the group so that other children and objects are out of reach.

Research (Kohn, 1999) shows that children tend to follow rules more consistently when they are part of the process of making the rules. Just as teachers who announce rules to their classes involve children in discussions about rules, role-play what it looks like to follow each rule, and draw pictures of themselves following the rules, so do teachers who create rules with the class.

Setting Guidelines

Not all early childhood classes have a set of rules and punishments. We believe in a child-directed community, so we approach the issue of rules differently. With agreement from our students, we set up one class rule. The rule might be one of the following:

- ◆ Be self-controlled.
- ◆ Use good manners.
- ◆ Do the right thing.
- ◆ Treat others the way you want to be treated.

The class's one rule applies universally to most, if not all, situations that arise in the classroom. For example, when George and Jarrett are sharing a ball on the playground, the rule of "Do the right thing" means that they take turns, throw the ball as close as they can to one another, negotiate to see if rolling or throwing the ball is what they both want to do, and so on. That same rule applies as well when George and Jarrett are eating lunch together. This time, "Do the right thing" means chew with your mouth closed, throw away your trash when it is your turn, eat your food without playing, and so on. By having only one class rule, you and your students establish the way the classroom operates; that is, you set the stage for the interactions that go on all through the year. At different times throughout the school year, the class discusses their one rule and how it applies to different situations.

Sample Class Discussion
About Establishing One Class Rule

Teacher: It's time for us to talk about rules in our class. Rules help us remember how we act in this school. Some classes have a lot of rules and some classes have only one rule. Let's think about that for a minute. Do you think it would be easier to remember a lot of rules or just one rule?

Several children: *(in unison)* Just one rule!

Teacher: Okay, I can see how that would be true. If that is what you think, then we need to talk about what that one rule will be.

Sarah Jane: Don't hit nobody.

Teacher: That is something that we definitely do not want to happen in our class. Hitting hurts people, so we don't want any hitting. But let's think about this for a minute. If we make our one rule "Do not hit anybody," does that rule remind us of how to act toward each other all the time? Is it enough that we just don't hit each other?

Letisha: No, I don't want people pushing me either.

Josue: What about yelling at people? I don't want people yelling at me either.

Letisha: Okay, our rule could be: No hitting or pushing or yelling.

Teacher: You guys are doing some very serious thinking. You are coming up with a list of things you do not want people to do in this room. Can we agree that none of us want to be hit or pushed or yelled at? Let me see a thumbs-up if you agree with that statement. Okay, that is unanimous. *Unanimous* means that every single person in the room voted that we are not going to hit or push or yell at other people. But I'm still wondering if a rule that says three things we should not do is good enough. It reminds us of things not to do, but it doesn't really tell us what to do. One of my classes made the rule "Be self-controlled." Would that rule remind us not to hit? If you are being self-controlled, would you hit someone else?

Several children: *(in unison)* No!

Teacher: If you are being self-controlled, would you push someone else?

Several children: *(in unison)* No!

Teacher: If you are being self-controlled, would you yell at other people?

Several children: *(in unison)* No!

Teacher: So far, the rule "Be self-controlled" seems to take care of the things we don't want to happen in our room. Could "Be self-controlled" remind us of things to do? What do you think?

Carlyle: What's self-controlled?

Teacher: That's a good question. Self-controlled means that you control yourself, that you make good decisions, that you do what you are supposed to do. Self-control looks different in different situations. We would need to talk about what self-control looks like in different situations. Let's think about when we have these meetings . . . what would self-control look like in a group meeting?

Letisha: Sit still, don't bother the person next to you.

Teacher: That sounds good. Would self-control look the same way at recess?

Several children: *(in unison)* No!

Teacher: Well, we can talk about that later. What do you guys think about this "Be self-controlled" rule? It is one rule that we can try and see how it works.

Several children: *(in unison)* Yeah!

Teacher: Then let me see a thumbs-up if you think we should try the "Be self-controlled" rule. Okay, that is unanimous.

Some people are skeptical about giving this much power or control to young children. We suggest that they consider what children learn as they go through the process of establishing their own rules and trying to live up to them. And we ask them to consider a statement made by John Dewey, one of our greatest twentieth-century educators: "Nothing is more absurd than to suppose that there is no middle term between leaving a child to his own unguided fancies and likes, or controlling his activities by a formal succession of dictated directions" (1900/1990, p. 130). We do not let children set any liberal rule they can dream up or allow them to act any way they want to act. However, we do believe that they should be active in the process of rule-setting with our guidance.

Analyzing Needed Routines

Some teachers expect that all children understand what it means to line up. To the adult mind, this request is very straightforward, but the statement could mean different things to different children. One child might think of standing ramrod straight, hands straight at the side with no talking. Another child might think of grabbing a friend's hand in order to have a partner to walk with, while still another might think of rushing to be the first person in line. None of these ideas may be exactly what the teacher had in mind. This is one small example of why teachers need to develop routines and teach them to children, explaining reasons for routines, leading children through discussions and practices of both logistical and academic routines, and planning ways to remind children about the routines.

Before school starts, it is helpful to brainstorm all the things that you want children to do—the who, what, when, where, and why of the classroom.

> Routines are procedures that ensure the effective use of time and space. The regular daily routines, as well as those special routines and events that are particular to your class, help establish a structure for classroom life, and contribute to the positive sense of community.
> — *Toni S. Bickart, Judy R. Jablon, and Diane Trister Dodge, 1999*

The following are some necessary routines:

- going to the bathroom
- getting necessary supplies in the classroom
- coming to the group area
- leaving the group area
- lining up
- entering the classroom
- preparing to go home
- dealing with coats and jackets
- returning homework
- going to the lunchroom
- purchasing a hot lunch and carrying it to the table
- cleaning up after eating
- going to the playground
- gathering after playtime
- getting quiet
- taking turns talking
- cleaning up after center time
- following procedures for academic instruction
- keeping up with work for portfolios

Because there are so many routines in an early childhood classroom, it is imperative that things run smoothly and that children understand exactly what is expected of them.

When you teach routines early in the school year, you save many hours of repeating explanations about what you want students to do throughout the rest of the year, leaving you more time for instruction. Routines need to be explained precisely to children. Children learn routines as you introduce them in class meetings, then through reminders and offered support throughout the school year.

Teaching Routines

Once you've decided which routines you want to put in place, think about ways you might introduce these routines. One way is to gather children in the class's group area, then lead them through role plays or dramatize a desired behavior for the class.

Guiding children to role-play various routines is an effective way to teach them. Small groups of children can practice how they want to role-play a routine, or you can verbally guide children as they act out the routine.

When you dramatize the routine, you may want to add a touch of humor and exaggerate the dramatization. For example, say you're showing children how to get a lunch kit from the locker. Go to the locker, overexaggerate repeated tugs at the lunch kit, then whine to the class, "Teacher, I need help. It will not come out of my locker!" As the class chuckles, return to the group area and discuss with children the details of getting the lunch kit, such as turning it so it will easily slide out of the locker or waiting until your locker partner has his or her lunch kit before getting yours.

Careful explanations and practice help children understand what the routine entails. When you discuss the routine with children, it gives them a voice in the establishment of the routine, thus giving them ownership in the routine. If children think routines are just something that you dreamed up, they will not put much effort into following the routines. But if you explain the reasons for routines, and include children in these discussions, their involvement rises. Before school starts, plan the language you'll use to justify routines with children. The sample class discussion below presents a scenario of how one teacher handled this justification.

Sample Class Discussion
to Justify Routines

Teacher: When it is time for us to come in from the playground, I need to have some signal to let you know that it is time to line up. It is my job to signal you when it is time to go in, and I can't walk around to everyone and say that it is time to line up. It is not safe to leave people out on the playground by themselves. So what can I do? How can I let you know what to do?

Amanda: You could blow a whistle and we could come when we hear that.

Teacher:	That's one suggestion. I'm going to write "Blow a whistle" on this chart. What else?
Tyrell:	When my baby-sitter wants me to come in from playing outside, she yells really loud for me.
Teacher:	How do you feel when she yells really loud? Do you like that?
Tyrell:	No, I really don't like being yelled at.
Teacher:	Then let's not put that on our chart. I don't want to do things that you don't like. Does everyone agree? Okay, what else?
Kim:	You could wave your arms and we could come when we see that.
Teacher:	Hey, that is a lot quieter than blowing a whistle. This says, "Wave my arms." That gives me another idea. I could walk to our lining-up spot. When you see me going in that direction, you could meet me there.
Children:	Yeah, we could do that.
Teacher:	Okay, this says, "Walk to lining-up spot." Any other ideas?
Johari:	No, I think the best one is to walk to the lining-up spot. That way we can see you walking and it gives us a chance to get there. If you blow a whistle or wave your arms, you'll be there before we are.
Teacher:	Does everyone agree to try this idea? We can see how it works this week and talk about it again on Friday. We'll save the chart until then. Is that okay with all of you?

The teacher clearly stated her reasons for the routine and solicited the children's help in finding solutions to the problem. She extended each child's suggestion, checking to be sure it was acceptable to all the children. While the children did not vote to accept or reject the ideas, she got a feeling of consensus from the group. Finally, she gave them time to practice the routine and evaluate its effectiveness.

Planning Ways to Offer Reminders

After you've decided on ways to introduce routines, you'll also need to consider how to support children's early attempts at following routines. Most children do not deliberately misbehave—they are just acting like the young children they are. When offering reminders, remember that children's sense of ownership is more important than a criticism of their behavior.

Offering a reminder before the routine is used is effective. You might say, "It is time to go to lunch. I remember that we decided to let the people who are buying their lunch go first, then the people that need to go to their lockers go. We decided this because the doorway was too crowded when we all went at the same time. Can the people who are buying their lunch please stand up? Do you have enough self-control to do this job? Okay, show the other people your best behavior."

At other times, asking a child or a group of children to dramatize a routine is effective. You might say, "I noticed that Jorge knows how to snap the lid back on the markers. Jorge, will you show the class how to push until you hear the snapping sound?" Jorge then gets a marker and shows the class the procedure.

Including all the children in the reminder is effective, too. You might say, "Think in your brain about all the things we need to do to get ready to go home. Tell the class what you are thinking about." Then, as the class rephrases the established routine, make sure that everyone remembers the procedure.

Thinking through rules and routines is an important part of preparing for the school year. Just as there are many aspects of routines to explore and to make decisions about before school starts, there are also issues relating to the classroom's arrangement to plan for. By doing this before school starts, you will be better prepared for the first day of school.

Arranging Classroom Furniture

During that week or two before the school year begins, the way classroom furniture is arranged may not seem very important. When you are the only person in the room— or when a teacher friend or two visit as you are setting up the room—it doesn't really matter how the tables are arranged or where the learning centers are placed. This changes dramatically when a whole group of young children joins you on that first day of school.

Young children view classrooms differently than adults do. It is clear that children are much smaller than adults, but many times teachers forget this obvious difference when they arrange their classrooms. Good early childhood educators look at the classroom from the point of view of young children and create a child-centered environment before the first day of school.

Too much furniture crowds students together. This makes it difficult for children to behave positively and purposefully.
— Marlynn Clayton, 2001

The way classroom furniture is arranged supports children's behavior. If the math materials are located in several parts of the room, children will wander around the room looking for what they need to complete assignments. If insufficient space is left between tables, children will bump into other chairs when they move their chairs or bump into each other as they are leaving their places at tables. If there are long open spaces in the classroom, many children will run from place to place. Put careful thought as to where furniture is placed in the room to prevent these behaviors.

Consider Children's Developmental Characteristics

One of the first things we consider when setting up our classrooms is the developmental characteristics of the children who will "live" in that room. (See "Young Children's Developmental Characteristics," page 24.) Knowing that young children learn best through active involvement with learning materials and with each other, we create learning centers or interest areas where individuals can work or small groups of children can collaborate. Since young children are developing independence and a sense of responsibility, we create a supportive environment with learning materials and supplies organized so all children can access what they need without adult assistance. We know different children prefer different work spaces, so we offer a variety of places within the classroom where children may choose to work. There may be a few desks placed around the room, tables with chairs, or tables whose legs have been shortened so children can sit on the floor while working. There is always a basket of clipboards for children who prefer not to work at a table. We know that children like to make choices about their work, so we offer choices for them in small ways—such as storing a variety of writing tools and paper in a common place— as well as in larger issues—such as offering several learning experiences for children to choose among. The classroom's physical arrangement supports all of these choices.

Teacher Tip

First Impressions

Remember the old adage about first impressions? It applies here too. The view of your classroom from the door expresses what you value and want to be important in your room. Placing the bookshelves so they are clearly viewed from the door sends the message that literacy is valued in your classroom. Are your books displayed prominently? Children's names, photographs, and work on display throughout the room reinforce the fact that children are valued. How are children portrayed in your classroom?

Young Children's Developmental Characteristics

and Implications for Room Arrangement

Pre-Kindergarten/Kindergarten Children...	So Teachers Create...
are still developing large-motor control	well-defined paths between pieces of furniture
are still learning how to work in pairs and small groups	choices of areas where small groups can work together
learn through social interaction with peers	learning centers that can accommodate two to four children
develop many reading skills	print-rich environments with a number of books, poems on chart tablets, group-experience stories, and functional print
develop a sense of "togetherness" from shared experiences with classmates	a group area large enough for group music and movement experiences
use pretend play to work through social and emotional issues	dramatic play centers and choices of props
need concrete reminders about appropriate behavior	well-defined learning centers and organized, labeled materials
take pride in their work	multiple display areas for children's drawings, paintings, writing, and models

First Grade/Second Grade Children...	So Teachers Create...
like to work in pairs and small groups	choices of areas where small groups can work together
choose to work alone on some projects	choices of areas where individual children can work independently
develop more sophisticated reading skills	print-rich environments with books, poems on chart tablets, group experience stories, and functional print
are still learning organizational skills	well-organized materials and supplies that are easy for children to access and maintain
develop a strong sense of time	clocks that are easily visible in all parts of the classroom

Consider Children's Behavior

As we arrange the furniture before school begins, we also think about the less-than-desirable behaviors typical of young children. Many of those behaviors can be prevented simply by the way the furniture is arranged. Young children are fidgety people. When we create a group meeting area, we make sure that it is large enough for children to move without annoying others around them. This avoids arguments during group meetings.

Young children's conversations tend to get louder and louder over time, so we encourage them to work in learning centers or interest areas. Then the noise of children's conversations is dispersed throughout the room.

As children sit in chairs pulled up at tables, they often need reminders to "push your chair in when you leave the table," or "sit with your bottom in the chair." One way to minimize this problem is to lower the height of the table so children can reach the work surface while sitting on the floor. Often table legs can be adjusted to place tables at a lower height.

It is also important to have space in the classroom for individual children to work alone. Offer clipboards for children to take to "private places" in the classroom, or arrange centers to do double duty. Perhaps the art center could be arranged so that space is available at other times of the day. Whatever you decide, this is something you should think through before the first day of school.

Consider Sight Lines

There are other general guidelines to follow when deciding where to place classroom furniture. One is to arrange the furniture so that you can see the entire classroom and everyone in the room. Tall furniture should be placed against a wall so it does not block the view of any part of the room. Even children working in private spaces need to be visible. Teachers often "test" their classrooms by standing and sitting in different positions around the room to make sure the entire room is visible. It is a good idea to retest the room several times during the first week of school to confirm that you can observe all children at all times.

> *Teacher Tip*
>
> ### Double-Duty Furniture
>
> Look for ways to make the furniture do double duty. Use bookshelves as dividers between centers, arranging them perpendicular to the wall. Place your filing cabinet so it can be used with magnetic letters.

Consider Traffic Patterns and Flow

Imagine the direction that children will move in and the paths they will take throughout the room. This also affects how you arrange the furniture. For example:

- ◆ Will there be a bottleneck of children around the writing center as children get their writing supplies?

- ◆ When children put their things away in the morning, is there sufficient room for them to unpack their backpacks and a clear path to where they need to go next?

- ◆ When children line up inside the classroom, is there enough space for the entire line without it snaking around furniture?

- ◆ What other things do you need to consider?

Once your room is set up, think through a typical day's activities and visualize how children will move around the room. To help traffic flow, you may create some "one-way streets," or paths where children will all move in the same direction. As part of your class routines, teach children to move in one direction in particular areas to prevent crashes when children accidentally bump into each other and to avoid spills when children are carrying supplies.

Typical Kindergarten Classroom

In this sketch of a kindergarten classroom, it is obvious that the room is organized by learning centers and that the space for each center is set off by carpets or bookshelves. Clearly defined centers support young children as they learn behaviors that are expected of them as they work in different learning centers. The noisier centers—blocks, dramatic play, water play, and music—are grouped together, as are the quieter centers—reading, writing, and listening. Other learning centers include a math center, a science center, and an art center. There is also a large space where the entire class can meet together, as well as spaces for children's personal possessions.

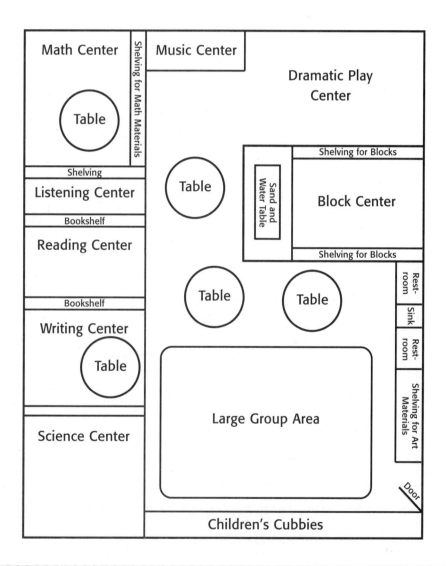

Typical Second-Grade Classroom

In this sketch of a second-grade classroom, the different spaces support different types of grouping. There are areas where students can work alone, with a partner, or in small groups. There is also a large area where the entire class can sit together for class meetings or other whole-group experiences.

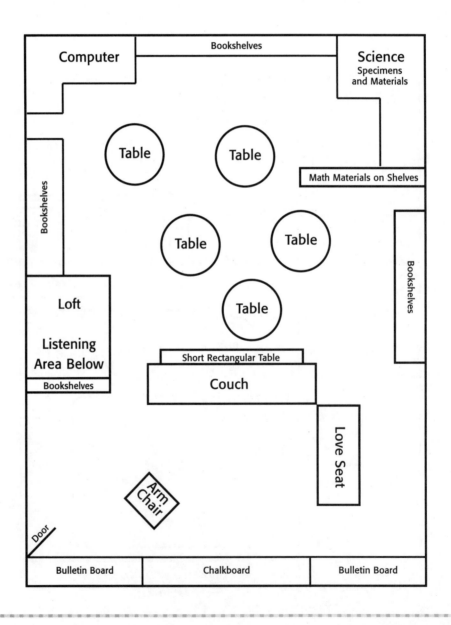

Rearrange the Furniture as Needed

Before school begins, you can only plan age appropriately. While you understand and make general plans for the developmental ranges of young children, the unique needs of the particular children in your class may require rearranging the furniture after the school year begins. One example that might require significant changes would be a child who uses a wheelchair for mobility. This situation would require more space between furniture than is usual in most classrooms. Supplies and learning materials might have to be reorganized so they are all accessible from a seated position. You might consider reorganizing the group area so all children bring chairs to the meeting area. That way everyone is at a similar height to the child in the wheelchair. Or you may find that most of the children in your class prefer to sit in chairs. Then you will need to rethink how the classroom chairs can do double duty. Can the chairs used at the tables be moved efficiently to the group area? Once in the group area, where will the chairs be placed?

Another reason for rearranging furniture would be for children who seem to need more space than others. You may have to change the arrangement of tables or desks to accommodate the child who "spreads out" all over the place as he works. If more children in your class prefer to sit on the floor to work, you might have to remove some of the furniture to provide extra work space on carpeted areas of the floor. The needs and preferences of the specific students in your class will guide your decisions about rearranging the classroom.

Comments
From a Kindergarten Teacher

I always set up my room in learning centers. This was my third year in the same room, so I didn't think much about setting up my classroom this year. I put the centers where they were last year—and the year before that. Then school started. Every day there were problems. I had a limit of two children in both the block and the puzzle centers, and those were the two most popular centers. The block center was a small center in one corner of the room. The space would not accommodate more than two children. The puzzle center was a child-sized table and two chairs, so only two children could go there. For two weeks, I listened to children argue about who could go to these centers first, then it dawned on me that I could take care of this problem by making these centers larger. I moved

Recycling "Found" Furniture

Recycled items often take on a new life when placed in the classroom. An upholstered chair that only needs a new slipcover can make a reading center for two children. Empty five-gallon ice-cream tubs turned on their sides and taped together can become cubbies to hold children's personal items. An old hat rack can be used to hold baskets of math manipulatives or other learning materials.

Furniture that offers a feeling of home can add to the classroom's atmosphere. We try to create a warm, nurturing environment in the classroom and believe that homey touches contribute to the feeling of comfortable surroundings. Placing a lamp in the reading center gives a soft glow to that area. An end table can accommodate science-center specimens and related books. A child-sized, square plastic table with two chairs makes a great place to work jigsaw puzzles.

Arranging classroom furniture is one of the easier tasks related to supporting children's appropriate class behavior. However, if this is overlooked or ignored, there may be problems related to students' behavior that could have been prevented.

Teacher Tip

Used Furniture

There is a fine line between dragging broken bookshelves off the curb and recycling used items. Before you haul it to school, make sure that used item will be an asset to your classroom. Can it be painted? Can it be turned sideways to serve another purpose? Will it add to the classroom's atmosphere? If the answer is no, leave it— no matter how tempting it may be!

Organizing Class Materials

Children's behavior is also affected by how easy or difficult it is for them to find the things that they need. When materials are logically organized, labeled, and within reach, there are fewer arguments among children. They also spend less time wandering around the room looking for something they want or need. This looking-for-something behavior often turns into unfocused behavior, which often results in the misbehavior of bothering other students in the class. You can prevent these behavior problems by carefully planning and implementing some organizational strategies.

Before the school year begins, think about how you are going to organize different kinds of materials in the classroom. What kinds of containers will you use for math manipulatives and science specimens? Could color-coding containers for different learning centers help children remember which materials should be returned to which center? Will children keep personal supplies or will the class use community supplies? Will baskets or plastic containers hold writing supplies? Will you label the place on a shelf for each container and use words or pictures, or both?

Having a plan that you've thought through before school starts is much easier than trying to figure out what to do as you add materials to the room from week to week. So, before the school year begins, we think about what types of materials and supplies will be used in the classroom and how they will be organized for children.

> There's no one right way to create an orderly and predictable classroom. What's important is that you create systems of organization that make sense to you and the children.
> — *Marlynn Clayton, 2001*

Teacher Tip

Start Small

At the beginning of the year, consider starting with only a few learning materials: only enough books in the reading center for each child in the class to have one book, only two types of paper along with pencils and crayons in the writing center, one book/audiotape in the listening center, two different types of manipulatives in the math center, one class pet and a collection of seashells in the science center.

Containers for Organizing Materials

- **Clear plastic containers**, approximately the size of a shoebox, with colored lids are good containers for math manipulatives and science specimens. They stack well, are easy to label, and the fact that they are see-through helps children find what they are looking for.

- **Baskets** of different shapes, textures, and sizes add aesthetic touches to the classroom, as well as organize materials. These baskets often have a handle and young children can easily carry the materials around the room.

- **Square, colored plastic containers** provide efficient ways to store materials. They usually stack, are easily labeled, and come in a variety of sizes. These can be placed in a corner or on a shelf.

- **Colored stacking bins** extend the storage area of the classroom. Because they have an opening along the front of the bin, children can return math materials or other small objects easily to the right place. Also, they sometimes come with casters, creating a rolling cart.

- **Colored plastic baskets** are a mainstay in many classrooms. Their rectangular shape can hold collections of books as well as materials for a learning center. They come in a variety of colors and lend themselves well to color coordinating. Interlocking circle clips fit between the spines of the baskets, allowing for easy labeling.

- **Colored plastic cups** can be used to organize small objects, like pencils or scissors. Placing color-coordinated cups inside a tote basket provides a place for small objects to be kept together. For example, a red tote containing two red plastic cups can be designated as the container for red-handled scissors.

- **Large plastic storage bins** can be used to store larger collections of objects, such as Duplos® or playground materials. These usually have tight-fitting lids and stack easily. Since two children can easily carry a bin, they can be used to transport supplies to different places around the school, such as gardening tools to the flower bed or playground equipment to the schoolyard.

Learning Materials

From the beginning of the year, children need enough learning materials so they can make activity choices and interact with different materials. But more important than choice is the issue of learning routines. We want children to learn to put materials back in their proper container and return the container to its place in the room. (See "Containers for Organizing Materials," page 32.) We believe in "a place for everything and everything in its place," and think it is important to explicitly teach that organizational system to our students.

When classroom materials are organized and children are responsible about using and caring for the materials, the materials last longer and many behavior issues are avoided. Fewer children trip over materials left on the floor. Fewer children argue over who gets to use which materials and when they can use them. More children can find what they are looking for.

> Too many available materials can make the environment overly stimulating. This can make it difficult for students to make purposeful choices and focus on their work.
> — *Marlynn Clayton, 2001*

Books

We begin the year by displaying only a few books, but we plan how we will display books throughout the year and suggest that you do this too. It does not matter how many books you have in the classroom if children cannot find them. The frustration children feel when they cannot find what they are looking for often leads to treating each other less than respectfully. Also, when children are unable to locate the book they want, they can become distracted and get off-task.

Some teachers use colored plastic tape to color-code classroom books by categories. You can find various colors of narrow

plastic tape in the electrical department of hardware stores. You can wrap a $\frac{1}{4}$ - by 2-inch piece of tape across the spine of the book, about one inch up from the bottom. For example, you might label all your poetry books with a piece of green tape spanning the spines of the books. Then all the poetry books can be easily spotted and grouped together on the same shelf. Since most classroom collections outnumber the available colors of tape, two or even three colors can be combined to represent one category. Attaching the tape to the book's spine also reinforces the idea that the books should be placed on the shelf with the spines facing out, so the tape is visible.

Supplies

Children's behavior also deteriorates when they cannot find the tool—crayon, glue, pencil, or whatever—they are looking for. If more than one child wants to use the same item, the behavior can lead to pushing or arguing. The way that supplies are organized can eliminate many off-task behaviors and arguments among children.

Teacher Tip

Organizing the Class Library

While there is no single best way to organize the books in a class library, these are some typical early childhood categories:

- ABC Books

- Animals

- Counting Books

- Cultures

- Dictionaries

- Different Languages

- Fairy Tales

- Families

- Guided-Reading Levels

- Magazines

- Math

- Newspapers

- Plants

- Poetry

- Predictable Texts

Comments
From a Second-Grade Teacher

My second graders needed a place for their markers, pencils, colored pencils, rulers, composition books, texts they were reading, and extra paper. After struggling with several ideas, we decided to use a large plastic tote to hold the smaller items and a milk crate-sized carton to hold the books. I covered some soup cans with contact paper that matched the color of the tote. These organized the scissors, markers, etc. The children stored both containers under their table. This cut down on movement around the classroom because each child only had to look under the table to find needed supplies.

Some teachers place supplies such as felt-tip markers, crayons, and pencils in small baskets on each table. Community collections of supplies keep arguments or accusations about "you took my marker" to a minimum. Store tools that are needed frequently, but not repeatedly, nearby. Place scissors in baskets that are color-coordinated with the scissors' handles for easy identification and cleanup, and store them in several locations around the room. Rulers can be color coordinated and stored in the same places. When children use individual supplies, they can keep them in cloth pouches that can be tied to the backs of chairs or in small plastic pencil boxes that slide under desks or tables.

Comments
From a First-Grade Teacher

I was so tired of all the arguments over whose No. 2 yellow pencil this is or who brought which sparkly pencil from home, discussions about why some children have pink and gray markers and other children don't, and accusations over who left the caps off whose markers. More importantly, it seemed fundamentally unfair that children didn't have equal access to writing supplies. Children whose families had more disposable income got new markers, crayons, and pencils when they

Comments (continued)

asked for them. Children whose families were struggling financially had to make do with what they had. After talking to lots of teachers, I decided to try having community supplies. At the beginning of the year, I pooled the items from the supply list. Everyone shares everything, and we bring out new supplies as needed. I've found that there are fewer arguments when children share supplies instead of each child keeping their own personal supplies.

I think this helped the way children in my class treat each other, too. It seems like sharing the supplies makes them more willing to participate in shared activities, like partner reading or working together on a math activity.

Arranging furniture and organizing supplies in effective ways support the classroom routines and learning that go on with the children. While there is no "right" way to do this, effective teachers think through and plan for as many situations as possible. Anticipating and preventing problems will help the first day of school, and subsequent weeks of school, flow more smoothly.

Summary

The time you spend considering class rules and routines is time well invested. Knowing what you expect from children and how you will go about encouraging positive behaviors allows you to start the school year as a strong leader of your students. The time that you spend creating a physical environment that supports children's appropriate classroom behavior is also time well spent. Many appropriate behaviors can be encouraged and many inappropriate behaviors can be prevented when the room is arranged in certain ways.

CHAPTER 2

THE FIRST DAY OF SCHOOL:

Setting the Tone for the Year

Before they can learn academics, they need time to learn to trust, to feel like somebody cares, and to begin to learn that they are important.

— *Jane Perlmutter and Louise Burrell, 2001*

Experienced teachers often caution new teachers that the first day of school is the most important day of the school year. In many ways this is true. The first day sets the tone for the school year. Even young children quickly react to places and people, forming first impressions that influence their later actions and decisions. That is why it is important to spend considerable time thinking about what to do on that first day of school and how to go about doing those things.

Some of the first-day-of-school issues include how to greet children as they come into the classroom, what kinds of activities to offer them on that day, how to introduce students to class rules and routines, how to organize school supplies that children bring, and finally, how to begin modeling behaviors we want to encourage in our students. When enough time is spent thinking about and planning for these first-day issues, that day—and all the ones after it—will go more smoothly.

Teacher Tip

Volunteers in the Classroom

The first few minutes of the first day of school are inevitably chaotic. It is a good idea to have another person—or two—in the classroom so that you can focus on greeting each child as he or she comes into the room. If the school cannot afford to hire a substitute teacher to work as extra help on the first day, perhaps you can convince a friend to volunteer for a few hours. If you cannot find an adult to help, you might consider recruiting two responsible students from an upper grade.

Greeting the Children

The moment children enter the classroom on the first day of school, kneel or bend over so you are at children's eye level. Look directly in each child's eyes, smile, and say a few words of welcome. Express pleasure that each child is in your room this year. Simply saying, "I am so happy that you are in my room this year,"

goes a long way toward helping a child feel a sense of belonging with this class. Watch the body language of the child and make appropriate responses to that, such as, "You look happy to be here today. Have you visited this school before?" or "Are you worried? I was a little worried about this day too, but there are a lot of interesting things to do here. Why don't you join Sarah? She's playing with the playdough."

Young children are better behaved in places where they feel psychologically safe. Aggressive behavior can often be traced to feelings of "not belonging." So by warmly greeting each child, making sure each one understands you are happy about his or her individual presence, introducing children to each other, and engaging each student in an activity with another student, you help children begin to feel that they belong in this class.

> When children feel safe—when they feel that they belong and are significant—they thrive. When children believe they do not belong and are not significant, they adopt survival (defensive) behavior...often called misbehavior.
> — *Jane Nelsen, Lynn Lott, and H. Stephen Glenn, 2000*

Comments
From a First-Grade Teacher

I knew you could pretty much count on a few criers on the first day of kindergarten, but I didn't really expect that to happen in first grade. Last year was a big exception. I had two children who were dropped off by older siblings after riding the bus to school. Both were sobbing uncontrollably. One was a boy, one a girl. Neither of them spoke a word of English. I was at a loss as to what to do. I hadn't planned on this and I hadn't had to deal with it before. In the confusion of so many children with so many needs, I forgot that young children need to feel safe. While they could not understand my words, I know they understood the tone of what I said as I held them in my arms and whispered to them that this was a good place to be, that I was their new teacher and that I would keep them safe. It took several minutes for their sobs to quiet down, but in those minutes, those children learned that I cared about them. And I think the other children who watched as I held two of their classmates learned that I cared about them as well.

Offering Engaging Activities

From the first few minutes of the first day of school, children need to gain the sense that there are interesting things to do in this classroom. Young children who are actively engaged in a simple learning experience are much less likely to exhibit inappropriate behaviors. By offering an engaging, interesting activity from the moment they step into the classroom, children see that this room is a place where learning is important and that they are expected to be participants in that learning. And while students are actively engaged in some kind of learning experience, you can spend time greeting each child as he or she arrives at the classroom door.

There are different factors to consider in selecting an activity—or two if you want to offer a choice—for children to do in those first few minutes of the first day of school:

◆ The activity should be one that different children can approach in different ways. Children of differing ability levels need to be successful in the activity.

◆ The activity should be one that encourages children to remain in the same place for the given time. Exploring the new room can be quite enticing to young children who are not engaged in an activity.

◆ Finally, the activity needs to be one that can be easily and quickly cleaned up.

As an example, having a few baskets of books available for children to peruse meets these factors. Most children have had experiences of leafing through books and know how to do this. As children choose their own book, they will be active, turning the pages and looking at the illustrations, and they do not need to know how to read to be successful. Books can be put back into their baskets rather quickly.

On the other hand, puzzles would not meet the factors for a good first-day activity. Unless 20-plus puzzles were available, some children would be observers instead of actively involved in working on one of the puzzles. Puzzles are closed-ended activities, so there is only one way to put them together. Children of different abilities may not put the pieces in the proper places, so some children will not be successful. Finally, one thing a teacher does not need to cope with on that first day is pieces from multiple puzzles scattered all over the floor. Careful consideration of first-day activities will avoid situations like the puzzle dilemma and help the day go more smoothly in general.

Suggested Activities for the First Morning of School

Pre-Kindergarten and Kindergarten

The youngest children benefit from activities that are open-ended, easy to clean up, and appropriate for one child or several at the same time. If possible, select common activities that children will have had some prior experience with outside of school. We find these to be appropriate:

- **Independent reading of books** — Small collections of books arranged in baskets on each table can be quite inviting. There are many wordless or almost wordless books that even these youngest children can "read." Group books in small baskets with handles so one child can easily manage to move the basket to the storage area at cleanup time. Rotate the baskets among the tables throughout the first week of school.

- **Playdough** — A small amount of playdough put at each child's place can entice even the most reluctant child. Provide resealable bags or easy-to-open cans for storage.

- **Interlocking cubes, such as Multi-Links**® — A small number of interlocking cubes placed in small baskets on each table offers open-ended play for children. Blocks that can be snapped together on different sides offer opportunities to construct all kinds of small representations. Avoid using blocks that only snap together in a linear fashion, as children quickly tire of that activity.

First and Second Grade

These children's prior school experiences guide your choices for the first-day activities. Talk to the previous year's teacher(s) and borrow familiar materials for the first-day activities. We find these to be appropriate:

- **Independent reading of books** — Group books together by themes and rotate the baskets among the tables throughout the first week of school. Possible themes could be families, beginning of school, dinosaurs, or other high-interest topics. Be sure to include books on different levels so all children are successful with the materials provided.

- **Pattern blocks** — This math manipulative is familiar to most children who have had school experiences. They will likely construct patterns or make shapes with the blocks. You can structure the activity by including patterns to cover, or offer mats with outlines of familiar shapes to fill in. Place these materials in small, shoebox-sized containers with a lid for easier cleanup. Be sure each child can reach the container of blocks easily. Provide two containers per table if necessary so children do not have to reach across each other to get more materials.

- **Interlocking cubes, such as Multi-Links®** — Older children enjoy creating representations with cubes as well as younger children do. Provide a sufficient number of blocks for children's more sophisticated constructions.

- **Crayons or markers for drawing** — If it is likely that children have had experience with crayons or markers, then these are appropriate for the first day of school. If you are unsure about their experiences, plan other activities. Dealing with a child who has written on the table (or another child's new clothes) is not something you want to address on the first day.

Comments
From a First-Grade Teacher

A beginning-of-school ritual for me is to make playdough. I've found that having playdough available for the children on the first day is a good way to start our day. I cook the homemade kind, shaping it into as many balls as I expect to have children (plus a few more). I store the balls in large resealable bags that I place on each table. After I greet a child and put on the name tag, I suggest that he or she find a place at a table and get a ball of playdough. When it is time to start the day, I ask children to roll their playdough into a ball and put it back in the bag. I keep some hand wipes ready for those children who need to wipe their hands after playing. This is an activity that most children like and that is easy to clean up. It makes for a smooth introduction to the first day of school.

Setting Class Rules

Young children find a sense of safety and security when they know what is expected of them. The first time an early childhood educator speaks to the whole class, she needs to communicate what children can expect of her and what she will expect from them. From our discussion of rules in Chapter 1, it is obvious that we believe young children should be a part of setting class rules or class guidelines. Of course, the paradox here is that rules or guidelines for behavior must be established very early in the school year, long before students have learned to make group decisions. In fact, many children will have had no experience in classrooms where their opinions are solicited, much less valued. So, your leadership in these early class discussions is very important. Lead the children's discussion in positive ways without taking over.

We find the techniques of reflecting, pondering, and wondering aloud (Diffily and Sassman, 2002) to be invaluable listening and questioning strategies in this situation. Restating a child's suggestion while remaining neutral about the content reflects the question back to the child. When the child hears her suggestion repeated aloud, she often tweaks it so it expresses exactly what she was thinking. This also puts the responsibility for the decision back with the children; we are merely repeating and reflecting what was said.

Sample Class Discussion
That Models Reflecting and Pondering

Teacher:	So, you don't like people pushing?
Taiyo:	No. We need a rule: "No pushing in line."
Teacher:	Is that what everyone thinks, that we should have a rule that says "No pushing in line"?
Danielle:	Well, it's not good to push anytime. Like at recess. That's not in line.
Teacher:	That is something to think about. What do you think?
Tonya:	But it's okay to push at recess, if you are pushing somebody on the swings.
Jeremy:	Yeah, you can push then, right?
Teacher:	Now, this is something to think about. Sometimes it is okay to push, like if you are swinging. Sometimes it is not okay to push, like when we are lining up. Do we need to think about this some more? Each person turn and face a partner. Touch your knees together and talk about how you think we should write this rule.

Pondering is a way to model deeper thinking about a question. It is a pensive, thoughtful response by the teacher that extends the comment made by the child. Comments such as, "How could we do that?" or "I wonder…" acknowledge the possibilities of the child's suggestion and support the child as he goes further with it. Hearing a suggestion repeated aloud often allows the child time to think about the suggestion and evaluate its pros and cons. It also encourages other children to consider a possible answer that may not have occurred to them.

Sometimes reflecting and pondering do not get at the heart of the subject. Instead of giving children the answer, we wonder aloud about the situation. We use this as an opportunity to model our thought processes for children. We might say, "We have to get to the cafeteria in order to eat our lunches. Is there some special way that we should do this?" Our body language conveys the idea that we are thinking about the situation and just talking out loud about it. We might raise a hand to touch the side of the head or slightly frown to indicate a wondering expression. By modeling our thought processes, rather than issuing an edict about a procedure, we are teaching children that their input is valued, that they have something valuable to say, and that we do not know all the answers. All of these things are important to a child's development as a learner.

Practicing Routines

Just as teachers share rules with children and have them practice what it looks like to follow a school rule, teachers also explicitly teach certain routines and have children practice those routines. Over the first few weeks of school, you will introduce many routines to children. Teaching too many routines on the first day is counterproductive. Children will feel overwhelmed, and most of them will not remember all the routines. On the first day of school, teach only two or three of the most important class routines.

One important routine for young children to learn is listening to other people—the teacher, other children, and other adults. This routine is used throughout the day—at group time, in different subject areas, and in situations that vary slightly. Children listen to other children during informal times, such as in the lunch line or when waiting to use the restroom, as well as in more formal situations, such as when the class is meeting in the group area. During the first group meeting of the first day, we teach children what to do to

show that they are listening to someone. We lead them through these steps several times and model the behavior ourselves:

1. Stop talking.

2. Turn your shoulders so that you are facing the person who is talking.

3. Make your eyes look into the eyes of the person who is talking.

4. Think about what they are saying while they are talking.

We choose different children to be the one speaking and talk about the fact that it is just as important to listen to their classmates as it is to listen to the teacher.

Another important routine to teach on the first day of school is stopping an activity and looking at the teacher. There will be many times during the first few weeks of school when we will need students' immediate attention, so we teach this routine and practice it many times the first day. We choose some kind of signal—striking a music wand, turning off the lights, turning a rain stick upside down, and so on—and introduce that as an important signal for children to "freeze" their action, turn their bodies toward us, and look directly at us.

Both of these routines are rather straightforward. Neither one includes children moving from one place to another or involves gathering materials for a particular learning experience. Those routines are a bit more complicated and should not be taught on the first day of school. Before we present those kinds of routines to children, we think them through, considering details such as:

- Will children have to cross in front of each other?

- Will two (or more) children bump into each other if they move that way?

- What will children do with their hands?

- What unique classroom features will enhance (or hinder) this routine?

- Is this an activity that lends itself to whispering (quiet talking or silence)?

- What supplies are needed?

- Where will they get the supplies?

- Can I facilitate this routine in some way (locating the notebooks in four small stacks instead of one large one, color-coding the folders for easier access, placing supplies on top of the table instead of in a drawer, and so on)?

We also want children to know that they have a responsibility in the development of class routines. So on the first day of school, we typically ask our students how they think we should carry out the routine. For example, when we lead discussions about how to walk in the hall, we say something like, "You know we have to walk from our room down to the cafeteria. We need to talk about what we will do when we walk in the hall. What things are important to remember when we walk in the hall?" We may take our students into the hall to watch how other classes do it, then ask them what they think. We hope our students will come up with suggestions such as:

- Walk on the right.

- Use a soft voice.

- Walk together.

- Leave a little space between you and the person in front of you.

If children do not make the suggestions that we think are important, we make pondering statements that lead children into agreeing to certain behaviors. We might say, "Do you guys think we ought to walk on the right side of the hall like the fifth graders we watched a few minutes ago? Does that sound like a good idea?"

Children can only bring to this discussion their past experiences and what they observed in the hall that morning. Many children will suggest how they were taught to walk in the hall in previous group settings. If a child comments, "You put one hand on your mouth and the other hand behind your back," we might comment, "Was that comfortable? Is that what you want to do at this school?"

After coming to agreement about several behaviors that we think are important to walking in the hall, we make a list of those behaviors, recording them on chart paper so all children can easily see the established behaviors. Because not all children are at the same developmental level, we also illustrate each behavior with a simple sketch. This illustration supports beginning readers and gives everyone a hint at what the expectation says.

Later that morning (after some active learning experiences, because young children should not sit for long periods of time), we bring children together for one more discussion of hall behavior, and create a rubric like the one in the photograph above. This rubric becomes our reference for the expected behaviors. Because a rubric details the desired and undesired behaviors, children can more easily evaluate their performance with it. We discuss what good behavior in the hall looks like and what not-so-good behavior looks like. We go back to the technique of modeling, asking a few children to model for the rest of the class what it looks like to have good hall behavior. Finally, we lead children as they practice the routine as a whole group.

After two or three days of practicing this routine, we return to the rubric, reread it to the class, and ask if there are changes that we should make in that routine.

Organizing Supplies

Typically, students bring school supplies to the classroom on the first day of school. Coping with bags of construction paper, glue, pencils, markers, and boxes of tissue can be challenging. Some teachers put all the bags in the back of the classroom and deal with supplies after students go home for the day. However, when children are part of organizing their supplies, they begin developing a sense of ownership of the classroom.

There are many ways to involve children in organizing supplies. Depending on the children's age, one way to begin is to first sort the supplies and then put them in the proper place. Get one bag of supplies from the back of the room, bring it to the group area, and

remove each item, placing it in a pile. Ask two children to get bags of supplies and do the same thing, adding supplies to each pile. One pile can be designated as the "talk about it later" pile for those objects that children bring that were not on your supply list. This frees you from answering questions about individual items and puts the responsibility for choosing a pile back with the child.

Older children can sort as they put items away. Using this method, take one bag of supplies and, as children are watching, place each type of supply in a different place; for example, pencils go into a plastic container on the writing-center table, crayons are removed from the box and placed in a different container on the same table, construction paper is stacked inside a cabinet where it will be stored for the year, boxes of tissues are put into the last cubbie/locker in the room, and so on. Then ask groups of children to be in charge of looking through the bags of supplies and finding one type of supply and placing it where it belongs.

Both processes will inevitably be a bit chaotic as children sort through supplies and go around the room. But it is worth a few minutes of disorganized activity to help children begin to develop the feeling that this is their classroom, and they are responsible for it.

Modeling Desired Behaviors

Throughout the first day, in every action and every interaction, keep in mind that you are modeling behaviors you want to encourage in your students. Even though the day may be hectic, consciously speak in a quiet tone of voice, use polite language, and generally act respectfully toward all children.

You cannot expect children to act in ways that you do not act yourself. If you want children to be calm, you must be calm as you teach the whole group, work with small groups, and interact with individual children. If you want children to speak in

> Teachers and administrators must model the social and academic skills which they wish to teach their students. These skills must be lived daily in educators' interactions with each other, with children, and with parents. Children are always watching.
> — *Paula Denton and Roxann Kriete, 1999*

quiet voices, you must consistently talk in a quiet, soft voice. A teacher's quiet, gentle manner is not only soothing, it also serves as a model for the ways that children interact with each other.

If you want children to use polite language—such as saying "please" when they ask for something and "thank you" when someone does something for them—you have to use this language yourself. Children who have not been taught this language at home often do not intentionally omit this language, they are just not aware of it. Your modeling may be the first consistent example the child has seen.

Too often teachers seem to forget that children deserve respect just as much as adults do, but if teachers want children to treat each other respectfully, they must interact with children respectfully. Respect can be shown to children in many different ways, such as:

- asking children to do things instead of making demands,
- acknowledging when children use polite language,
- expressing appreciation when children do what they are asked to do, and
- saying thank you when appropriate.

Comments
From a Second-Grade Teacher

I had to attend a before-school workshop for teachers. I had been teaching for more than ten years and certainly did not think that I needed some presenter to tell me how to begin the school year. I had the drill down pat. I knew how to set up my classroom, how to make students and their families feel comfortable on that first day, how to engage children in interesting learning experiences from the first few minutes of the day, and I was organized to the point of being anal. My attitude was not great when we all started the workshop that morning, but about half an hour into the morning session, the presenter began talking about teacher language and how what we say the first day of school sets the tone for the year. She asked us to spend about ten minutes writing down the phrases we used the first day of school, before lunch. As I

Comments (continued)

started making notes, it dawned on me that I was somewhat of a dictator with my class: "Sit here," "No talking," "Look at me," "Listen," "Stand up," "Don't move," "Line up." After we spent a few minutes sharing what we had written, the presenter asked us if that is how we wanted our students to interact with each other. Next, she challenged us to make a list of how we wanted our students to talk to each other. Then, she asked us to get into small groups and discuss how we might model those ways of interacting with other people in that first day of school. That hour of the workshop changed how I planned for my next first day of school. I was much more aware of how my behavior and how my words were the model for the way my class would be this year.

Summary

The first day of school sets the tone for the rest of the school year. Plan this day very carefully and implement those plans, from the words you will use to greet individual children, to the activities that you will offer to students, to rules and routines to introduce and practice. Throughout each activity and every group discussion, be mindful of the fact that you are the model for your students.

CHAPTER 3

THE FIRST WEEK OF SCHOOL:

Getting to Know Each Other and Establishing Basic Routines

During the first few weeks of school, children need to be involved in developing the schedules, systems, and expectations that will guide them throughout the year.

— *Jane Perlmutter and Louise Burrell, 2001*

Just as the first day of school sets the tone for the school year, the first week sets up the routines for the year. Continue to do what you introduced on the first day, greeting each child at the beginning of the day, offering interesting learning experiences for students, and modeling positive behaviors. Expand on these concepts as well by organizing activities that help children begin to see each other as friends, encouraging them to take care of themselves and each other. Teach more and more routines, begin having different types of class meetings, and reinforce—not reward—appropriate behaviors. And, perhaps most importantly, begin the process of getting to know each child individually and meeting as many needs for each child as possible.

Comments
From a Second-Grade Teacher

Last summer a friend of mine and I decided to gather a group of teachers to study the idea of creating a sense a community in our classrooms. We talked to lots of teachers and put together a reading list. In three months, we read six books and met every two weeks to talk about what we were reading. The books were:

Among Friends
by Joan Dalton and Marilyn Watson

Beyond Discipline: From Compliance to Community
by Alfie Kohn

Moral Classrooms, Moral Children
by Rheta DeVries and Betty Zan

Positive Discipline in the Classroom
by Jane Nelsen, Lynn Lott, and H. Stephen Glenn

Teaching Children to Care: Management in the Responsive Classroom
by Ruth Sidney Charney

Ways We Want Our Class to Be
by Child Development Project

One strategy that seemed to be integral to all of these authors' opinions about creating community was the use of class meetings. I had never done this with my students before, and I'll admit, I was a bit skeptical. But we all agreed to try class meetings for the fall semester and meet again over the winter holidays.

It was amazing to sit in that late December meeting and listen to all the stories about how class meetings positively affected children in these classes. Children were more respectful toward each other. They cared more about each other. Everyone's class was just running more smoothly.

Becoming Friends

Many children begin the school year not knowing anyone else in the class. Teachers are aware that many children understand very little about how to begin making friends with virtual strangers. During the first few days of school we spend a lot of time helping children see themselves as friends.

One very simple strategy to use is calling children by their names. When students hear us use their names over and over, they begin remembering each other's names. Knowing someone by name is a small step in feeling like they are friends.

When we address the whole group of children, we use the term *friends*, instead of referring to them as boys and girls or students. Again, this is a very small thing, but over several days, children pick up this term. Often when they cannot remember a classmate's name, they will use the term *friend*.

Additionally, we explicitly tell children that in this class we are going to be friends. We tell them that we may not always like everything that other people do, but that we will all treat each other respectfully and help each other, because that is what friends do.

Teacher Tip

Helping Children See Themselves as Friends

- Help children know and use each other's names.

- Assign partners for learning experiences.

- Model how to make room in the circle for children who are late in joining the circle.

- Create class rituals such as a beginning-the-morning song or poems used for transitions.

Teacher Tip

Activities to Help Children Learn Each Other's Names

There are many class activities that help children learn each other's names. In *Classrooms That Work: They Can All Read and Write*, Patricia M. Cunningham and Richard L. Allington outline several activities, including the following:

- **Special Child:** Write all the children's names on sentence strips, putting long names on long strips and short names on short strips. Each day, draw a name from the collection. That child becomes the "King (or Queen) for the Day," and the child's name becomes the focus of many activities.

- **Special Child Book:** Each child in the class writes the special child's name on a piece of construction paper. Then they interview that child to discover his likes and dislikes, pets, favorite foods, and other details. Then each child draws a picture about the special child. Collect and assemble the pages into a book for the day's special child to take home.

- **Longest Name/Shortest Name:** Using the sentence strips from the "Special Child" activity, children count the number of letters in each name. Then place the strips in a pocket chart in order from shortest to longest and longest to shortest. Group together names with the same number of letters.

- **Graph the Names:** After counting the letters in each child's name, transfer that information to a chart or graph. This can be posted in the classroom.

- **Be the Name:** Write each letter in a child's name on a separate index card. Distribute cards to children in the class. Challenge them to arrange themselves to spell the given child's name by standing in the front of the room as they display their cards.

- **Rhyme the Name:** Many short names can easily be rhymed. Or the class can compose a short rhyming poem about that child: "My friend is Jake; he likes to eat cake."

We organize different learning experiences where children work together in pairs or in small groups. When children are working toward a mutual goal—drawing a picture together, playing a game, looking through a book to find a certain object in the illustrations—they make a personal connection with other people and begin developing friendships. After multiple learning experiences with different partners, most of the children in the class are beginning to view many of their classmates as friends.

Offering Interesting Activities

Even young children spend more time with and learn more from activities that they choose themselves. Early childhood educators realize the importance of child choice and carefully balance the day with engaging group experiences and choices of interesting learning center activities.

At the beginning of the school year, you'll want to limit the time that you ask young children to sit during large-group activities. Group activities—read alouds, echo reading of poems, class discussions, role-playing, finger plays—for kindergartners and first-grade students are best kept to less than ten minutes. You can increase this time as children become accustomed to you and their classmates and as their attention spans become longer. But during the first week of school, it is important to keep children in large-group activities only as long as they are engaged. As soon as two or three children begin fidgeting, bring closure to that group activity and switch activities.

At this point, you can change the passive nature of most large-group activities to more active group activities, such as moving to action songs or other large-muscle activity—or you can dismiss students to individual or small-group learning experiences. We are very explicit about the behaviors we expect as the children leave the group activity. We give clear, concise directions so children know exactly what is expected of them, and we have the opportunity to stage the movement in a controlled manner. In this way, children know where to go and what to do instead of having to make judgments or decisions about how to move about the classroom.

Comments
From a First-Grade Teacher

It was my first year of teaching, and transition time was when children usually got out of hand. After talking with a veteran teacher, I realized that I was giving directions that were too general and vague. These young children needed to know exactly what I wanted them to do. So now I start out the year saying, "Get a pencil from the basket at your table and write your name on the line at the top of the page" instead of "Write your name on the paper." Being more specific really helped a lot.

When you dismiss children from the large group to small-group activities, you need to be very explicit about what you expect children to do during this time. Moving from one place to another in a new room is hard for young children. They may not remember which bookshelf contains the math center or where the scissors are stored, so they wander around the room, truly thinking they are doing what you asked. One way to help facilitate this movement is for one or two children to model the desired behavior for the class. While the desired behavior is being modeled, direct the behavior, reiterating and reinforcing the positive things that happen. After the modeling is completed, dismiss five or six children to carry out the movement, and then let the rest of the class move. Controlling the number of children that are moving at one time lowers the possibility for misbehavior.

When you dismiss children to individual activities, be explicit about the choices that children have. In most kindergarten or first-grade classrooms, individual choice time usually means children choose the learning center where they want to work. At the beginning of the year, wise early childhood educators offer only one or two, maybe three, activity choices in each learning center. Too many choices overwhelm some children.

One way to deal with choosing between activities is to ask the child to select an activity from the possible choices before he leaves the group area. That way, when the child reaches the learning center he knows what he wants to do and can begin to do that activity. Some teachers approach this as having children "make a promise" about what they choose to work on. Young children are conscientious about keeping a promise and understand this concept. Then, as children reach their learning centers, they know what they have chosen to do, and they begin that activity.

Taking Care of Ourselves

From the first week of school, reinforce the fact that children can take care of themselves and that you expect them to do that. Many young children have developed a sense of learned helplessness before they start school. When parents or caregivers attend to a child's every need, the child learns over time that adults are the ones who are supposed to solve problems. They just do not see themselves as capable.

Many children are taught to ask permission for everything they want to do. Parents who teach their children to do this do not realize that this is detrimental to a child's sense of competency. We are not suggesting that young children be allowed to do anything they want, but there is certainly no reason that children should feel they have to ask to get a tissue when they need one.

One way that we help children with this is by our genuine response to their inquiry. When a child asks permission to do a task or get something that he is capable of deciding about or getting, we kindly respond, "That is a decision you need to make." This simple

Responsibility and reliability and trustworthiness can be taught quietly ... Some (ways) are as straightforward as learning to sew on a button or to get up on time. Others are as complex as what it means to cheat on a test or lie to a friend.
— Dorothy Rich, 1997

response puts the child back in control and gives him permission, even encouragement, to make decisions independently. Other responses are more of an inquiry: "What do you think?" or "Is that something you want to do?" Along with this, we also begin to refer children to other children for help.

When children do not see themselves as capable, they certainly don't see their peers as a source for help. One adult in a classroom filled with young children cannot help every child every time they need something. Children can and should help each other. They can tie each other's shoes, find lost items, zip jackets or coats, or locate a certain color marker or crayon.

You can purposefully emphasize this idea of "taking care of yourself" by the language you use with children. Responses like, "I'm not sure, what do you think?" or "Hmmm, what could be done about that?" return the responsibility back to the child. You'll always be available for support and to offer suggestions, but you lead the child into discovering how to accomplish the task on his or her own.

Practicing More Routines

Most likely, you've already introduced two or three routines on the first day of school. Each day of the first week, practice those routines again and introduce new ones. For each routine, have children practice the behavior, demonstrating the correct way to go through that particular routine. Since the whole class participates together in this practice, children continue to develop a sense of community. That is, children begin to feel they are a group, a successful group mastering particular skills.

Teacher Tip

Helping Each Other Charts

One way to assist children to consider each other as sources for help is to create charts. During the first week of school, title a posterboard, "I Can Help You." Then, as they occur during the class's activities, add competencies that children can do, such as posting the statement "I tie shoes" with the name of the child who can tie shoes beside it. Then when a child asks you to tie his shoes, you can refer the child to the list on the posterboard. Help him choose a classmate who can tie shoes.

Other competencies can be added as you notice them; for example, "I can take the lid off the baskets," "I can fix the stapler," "I can untangle the jump rope," and so on.

Comments
From a Kindergarten Teacher

It seems like I forget from year to year. Each year, after that first day of school, I think, "Wow, this is the most well-behaved group of students I've ever had." I think the same thing the second and third days of school, but then somewhere around the end of the first week or beginning of the second week, that honeymoon period ends. I start seeing the children's real personalities and their typical behavior. That is the moment when I am glad that I started laying the groundwork, explaining exactly what I expect from children and helping them internalize routines.

There is not a definitive list of routines that each early childhood class needs. However, several situations run more smoothly when specific expectations are taught to children. For example, as children arrive at school in the morning they need to put away their personal belongings and do what is needed to begin the day. In one first-grade class where the children's lockers were located in the hallway outside the classroom, the teacher taught this routine:

1. When you turn down the hall by the classroom, go straight to your locker. Open it.

2. Put your backpack on the floor, unzip it, and take out your lunch. Put your lunch on the top shelf.

3. Take out your daily work folder and your take-home reading folder.

4. Bring those two things with you as you enter the classroom. Leave your backpack on the floor, near your locker.

5. Place the daily work folder on your table and replace the book in your take-home folder with a new one.

6. Take the take-home folder and new book back into the hallway, to your locker.

7. Put them in your backpack. Zip the backpack closed. Use the loop at the top to hang it on the hook in the locker.

8. Close the locker and return to the classroom.

9. Select a before-school activity from the choices provided.

Within this routine, there are other specific routines that the teacher addressed with different children. Some children had trouble selecting a new book while they had the take-home folder in their hand, so she developed a separate procedure for that. If several children arrived at the lockers at the same time, the floor was littered with backpacks and other children could not pass by. Again, she developed a separate procedure for standing the backpack on its end against the locker's door. Other children needed help learning how to turn the handle and pull at the same time to open the locker, zip the backpack, turn their lunch kit so it fit in the top space, and so on. Each routine calls for more than is obvious at first glance.

Some typical routines are described in the Teacher Tip box on page 62. This list offers a few examples, certainly not all the routines that need to be developed for an early childhood class. None of the descriptions expresses the only way to accomplish the routine. The steps in any routine depend on the children, the arrangement of the classroom, the layout of the school, and your preferences.

Typical Routines for Early Childhood Classrooms

Going to the Bathroom: Look on the wall to see if the Boy/Girl tag is hanging on the wall. Get the correct tag. Leave the room without talking. Walk quietly to the bathroom. Hang the tag on the hook in the bathroom. After you use the bathroom, wash your hands with soap and water. Dry your hands with a paper towel. Throw the paper towel away in the trash can. Remember to bring the tag back to the classroom. Hang the tag back on the wall in its place. Return to the group or what you were working on.

Reading With a Partner: Confer with your partner to agree on who will read first. Use one of the class's strategies (do Rock, Paper, Scissors; flip a coin; draw straws; and so on) if you cannot decide. Watch your partner as he reads. Help him remember the reading strategies if he gets stuck. Both partners are responsible for returning the books and other supplies to the proper place.

Working in a Small Group: Decide who is responsible for which job. Allow every group member to tell ideas. Listen to the person who is talking and make sure your response builds on that person's ideas. Be serious about your work and get the job done.
Note: Each team member within a group should have a job, and over time each student should have an opportunity to do each job. Develop job descriptions and routines for assigning the jobs. Jobs for a five-member group might be timekeeper, reporter, recorder, encourager, and materials manager.

Putting Work Where It Belongs: When your work is finished, double check to make sure your name and the date are on your paper. Put your tools (markers, pencils, glue, manipulatives, and so on) away. Stand up, pushing your chair under the table. Pick up your paper and walk to the basket on the math shelf. Put your paper on top of the other papers in the basket with the work facing up. Put the top of your work at the top of the basket. Return to your place or go to the next activity.

Teacher Tip (*continued*)

Having Snack: Stop what you are doing when the song "I Like to Eat" begins. Leave what you are working on where it is. Walk quietly to the meeting area. Sit down. Sing along while waiting for everyone else to sit down. Wait for snack helpers to give you a snack. Quietly eat the snack while the teacher reads. When finished, put your trash in the trash can. Quietly walk back to where you were working.

Cleaning Up: Check the floor around your desk. Pick up any trash and throw it away. Pick up any pencils or other objects on the floor and put them where they belong. Check the "Clean-Up Jobs" board to find out who your partner is and which job you are assigned to. Find your partner. Complete your job with your partner without bothering other students.

Getting Ready to Go Home: Get your "every day" folder and put it at your seat. Pick up one copy of all the papers on the "Take Home" table, then put them in your folder. Get your backpack, lunchbox, and coat from your locker. Put the "every day" folder in your backpack. Bring all these things to the group area and listen to the read aloud until the dismissal bell rings.

Teaching routines and practicing each one several times may seem quite time-consuming. This process does consume large blocks of time during the first few weeks of school, but making sure that everyone in the class understands what is expected of them saves lots of reminder discussions through the entire year.

Keep families informed about the established routines. Not only does this offer the family a glimpse

into what goes on in the classroom, but it also gives them a framework for discussions with their child. A parent who knows the procedure for arriving in the morning can better assist her child during that process. Include a discussion about routines in a family letter to introduce this idea.

Letter to Families
to Introduce Routines

Dear Families:

Routines are important in elementary classrooms. When all of the children know what I mean when I say, "Line up," or "Get ready to go home," the days run more smoothly. So we have lots of routines in our class.

I am careful to explain exactly what children should be doing at different times during the day. After I talk about a routine, we practice it until everyone in the class understands it. We have routines for putting personal things where they belong in the morning, coming to the group meeting area, lining up, going to the bathroom, getting a drink of water, going into the cafeteria, cleaning up after eating, getting necessary supplies in the classroom, cleaning up after center time, and getting ready to go home at the end of the day.

In the next few weeks, I will be teaching your children different routines that relate to reading, writing, and math learning. I will keep you posted on those routines, too.

I think young children find a sense of security when they have routines. They know what to expect. If your family doesn't already have some routines, you may want to think about setting up some at home, too; maybe a routine for getting dressed for school or going to bed at night.

Sincerely,

Beginning Class Meetings

Holding regular class meetings has multiple benefits for young children. Class meetings are times when you and your students join together to solve problems, plan activities, or share information. Class meetings help students begin to see themselves as a community where members exchange ideas and support each other. When differences are addressed and discussed by everyone in a class meeting, instead of having you impose a solution for the group, children learn that each member of their class is valued and important. As you and your children work toward consensus, they learn that there are many solutions to a problem, that other people's ideas might be better than their own, that collaboration is stronger than one person working alone, and that there are ways to get along with others.

How long should class meetings be? There is no single answer to this—it depends on the age and experience of the students, the topic(s) to be addressed, and the purpose of the meeting.
— *Child Development Project, 1996*

Students have a tendency to tune out of teacher-dominated meetings, so it is important that all participants have a voice during class meetings. This is not a time for you to lecture. Instead, you or your students bring up an issue that concerns the entire class, then everyone works together to evaluate the problem, deciding on a solution that most people think may work.

For this to happen, you and your students have to respect each other. There is no place in class meetings for making fun of other children, name-calling, or any other form of put-down. Model respectful language, but also help children understand what language is not acceptable in a class meeting. If put-downs begin, stop the statement and remind children about what kind of language is expected in class meetings. If one child begins to make fun of another, explain that that language is not acceptable and that no one can make fun of anyone else.

Class meetings are also a time to develop a sense of cooperation among students. When children are involved in meetings that set the tone for the day, where they plan their day, make decisions together, and learn to solve conflicts, they come to believe that they can cooperate and do all kinds of important things.

Morning Meetings

Some early childhood educators have adopted the Responsive Classroom approach to class meetings, which always starts the day with the class gathered together for morning meeting (Kriete, 1999). This type of meeting has four basic components: greeting, sharing, group activity, and news and announcements.

Believing that children need a predictable way to start the day, teachers who adopt this approach implement the same four components in the same order every day. The greeting may change some. One day the class may clap, the next day, sing, and the next day, shake hands with each other, but every day the greeting incorporates children greeting each other by name. Some days, sharing may be a pair-share; other days, only two or three children may share, but sharing always follows the greeting. The group activity may be a group song, a choral reading of a poem, or a role-play, but the whole class always participates in a short activity together. Finally, the group spends a few minutes reading and discussing a daily message that the teacher posts.

The most important thing about morning meeting is not what occurs in each of the four components. The most important purpose is how it sets the tone for the day and supports a climate of trust between you and your students. This tone and climate extend throughout the day, and this helps meet two important human needs: the sense of belonging and the need to have fun (Kriete, 1999).

Some teachers have personalized the morning-meeting structure for their classroom. The routine is still predictable and children are active participants in the activities. But they may begin by saying the Pledge of Allegiance or singing a good-morning song. Sharing the day's calendar may follow, or the school-wide announcements may come next. No matter what morning routine you establish, it is important to remember that it occurs at the same time every day and that this is not a time for you to do all the talking.

> The time one commits to Morning Meeting is an investment, which is repaid many times over. The sense of belonging and the skills of attention, listening, expressing, and cooperative interaction developed in Morning Meeting are a foundation for every lesson, every transition time, every lining-up, every upset and conflict, all day and all year long.
> — *Roxann Kriete, 1999*

Comments
From a Kindergarten Teacher

As a kindergarten teacher, I have always started the school day by meeting with all my students. We would sing songs, do finger plays, read books, and talk about what we were going to do that day. After listening to some friends, I changed the focus of what I used to call "circle time." Now we have "morning meetings" and begin our days talking about important things.

Planning Meetings

Group meetings can also be used to make plans—plans such as deciding about and organizing the day's work, introducing and modeling a social skill, presenting a new game or set of materials, or talking about longer-term plans for a class inquiry.

Children work more purposefully when they have a plan for the day. The High/Scope program suggests a "plan–do–review" approach for young children's work. This approach suggests that teachers ask children what they plan to do during each learning center time and keep notes about children's plans. Then after their work time, teachers ask children to talk about how their work went. This same framework is suggested for early childhood writing workshops. After you give a short lesson, children announce what they plan to write about, then spend a block of time writing, followed by a sharing time when they share their writing. This approach to children's work serves as a model for planning meetings.

Generally, planning meetings follow this format. You and your children discuss the problem at hand, outlining possible solutions. Agree on a way to accomplish the task, then work toward that accomplishment. When work time is over, gather together again to review the accomplishments and briefly outline the plans for the next step.

> The strength of a morning meeting depends on the capacity of children to take responsibility for the routines of the group: active listening, relevant comments, enthusiastic play, sitting still, raising a hand. There is a lot to learn.
> — *Ruth Sidney Charney, 1991*

Planning meetings can occur with the whole class or with small groups of children. When a small group's behavior is off task, move to that area, sit down with the children, and ask, "What's the plan here?" This is usually enough to redirect the children's attention away from the misbehavior and back to the task at hand. As children respond, repeat the needed tasks: "Okay, Jennifer and Jason are going to write down the math equations while Lonnie and Regina roll the dice. Are you all comfortable with that?" It is important to note that in this situation you did not ask for an accounting of the misbehavior, you simply got the children back on task.

Making Decisions Together

Some children come to school having had experiences in group decision making. Their families have modeled the process of group decision making: letting everyone in the group say what they think about an issue, listening to all sides, discussing pros and cons, and compromising. But usually, more children come to school without these experiences.

During the first week of school, teach children the steps in making group decisions. Many of the early class meetings will revolve around discussions about how children want the class "to be." The decisions that come from these discussions may be:

> Decision making is not easy, but it becomes less painful as children:
>
> ◆ become increasingly aware that they can help to solve problems.
>
> ◆ see that a problem can have more than one solution, but that one may be better than others.
>
> — *Dorothy Rich, 1997*

- ◆ We decided to listen to each other.

- ◆ We decided to help each other.

- ◆ We decided to be respectful and not to call each other names.

- ◆ We decided to be kind to each other.

These kinds of group decisions are not particularly difficult. Most children want to do the right thing, and are easily convinced that these behaviors are good ones for everyone in the class to do. More importantly, children are learning how to participate in a class meeting. They are learning to wait for their turn to speak, attentively listen to others, evaluate what is being said, and to put their immediate wants on hold for the greater good of the class.

Once these early class meetings have established guidelines for the class, the decision-making focus of meetings changes. Gradually introduce the concept that meetings can be used for different purposes but that the format and guidelines remain the same.

To reinforce making decisions together, we also offer many opportunities during the first week of school for children to make decisions. Some of these are as simple as presenting two books for the class's daily read aloud and asking children to vote on which one to read first. Other decisions could include what snack to have on Friday, how to line up for lunch, what game to play at PE time, and so on.

Resolving Conflicts

We find that many of the class meetings during the first few weeks of school focus on resolving conflicts. At the beginning of the year, we bring up conflicts in a generic way. We sometimes comment (in an astonished, unbelieving tone of voice) that in other classes, we've seen or heard about some problems with children hitting or pushing each other. That is generally enough to launch a conversation about how children feel when someone hits them and what they can do when that happens.

As a general rule, with young children, conflict-resolution meetings should be as concrete as possible and limited to a few minutes. "When discussing behavioral expectations with five- or six-year-olds, it is best to cite specific examples and use clear models. Structured role-playing, storytelling, or using puppets or flannel-board figures can help young students learn how to answer such questions as, 'How should we behave when someone isn't willing to share with us? How can we tell someone when we are angry without hitting or yelling?'" (Landau and Gathercoal, 2000, p. 452)

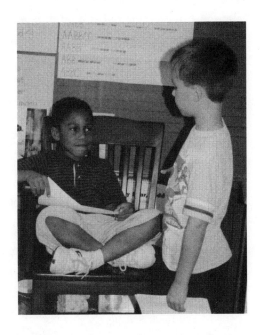

Conflicts are inevitable in an active classroom where free social interaction occurs. In many schools conflict is viewed as undesirable and to be avoided at all costs. Instead, we see conflict and its resolution as essential to a constructivist curriculum.
— *Rheta DeVries and Betty Zan, 1994*

> If self-controls are established at one point...it doesn't mean that problems, conflicts, and stunning bursts of impulse and disobedience will be erased.
> — Ruth Sidney Charney, 1991

When the class holds a problem-solving meeting, record the conversation. You might write the problem at the top of a piece of chart paper, then list suggestions as children offer them. When the class comes to an agreement about how they are going to handle a particular problem, record the agreement as well. Post the paper for reference or put it somewhere where it can be reviewed at a later date if the problem comes up again.

Class meetings that focus on resolving conflicts typically go through four separate stages:

1. Identify the problem.

2. Discuss the situation, expressing how we would feel if we were involved in that situation.

3. Brainstorm possible solutions.

4. Practice one or more of the solutions in role-play situations.

After a meeting or two, children are pretty good at identifying problems, especially in identifying how someone else has caused a problem. They are not quite as good at describing how they would feel or in brainstorming possible solutions. Children who have not been through this kind of process before often talk about two kinds of feelings: bad or mad. We work with young children, labeling what we believe their feelings may be—embarrassed, disappointed, and so on—so that they learn, over time, to label their own feelings. As the teacher, it is sometimes necessary to suggest possible solutions to problems. Rather than announce a solution to the group, we use language such as: "I wonder if we might think about..." or "Do you think that...could be a possible solution?" Again, over time, children will begin to use the language we model and will start offering their own solutions to problems presented to the class.

It is important to remember that class meetings are not

Teacher Tip

Solving Problems Chart

Sometimes it helps children to have a visual reminder of the steps involved in a conflict-resolution meeting, such as the following:

1. Define the problem.

2. Generate solutions.

3. Discuss solutions.

4. Reach an agreement.

5. Evaluate the solution in a later check-in meeting.

perfect when you first begin using them with young children. Many children who come into your classroom have never been in situations where they were asked to solve their own problems. If they have been in classes where the teacher was the person who solved all problems, then their tendency will be to repeat the kinds of behavior they had in those previous classrooms. If tattling was the norm, they will continue tattling for several weeks until they learn that things are "different" in this class. If they have been punished when they broke the rules in other classes, the solutions they offer for problems may be very punitive. However, over time children will learn appropriate language for class meetings and become functioning members of a group that solves problems together.

Teacher Tip

Possible Ways to Start a Class Meeting

- "I noticed something on the playground today that we need to think about. John and Richard (I have their permission to use their names) were playing hide-and-go-seek with some other people when Richard got tired of playing. When Richard walked off and started climbing on the overhead ladder, John went over to him and asked him if anything was wrong. What do you think about this? Is this something other people in our class should do?"

- "I am such a lucky teacher. You all make such an effort to get along with everyone. Last year's class never got along as well as you do. They would speak to each other in disrespectful tones. What is it about your behavior that makes the voice tone you use so pleasant?"

- "Did you see what the other kindergarten class did in the lunchroom today? They left paper on the floor and didn't wipe their tables. What can we do to make sure that doesn't happen with our class?"

- "I've got some bad news for you. Mrs. McGuire said that some children are playing behind the school before school starts. That is not appropriate behavior. So how can we make sure that no one in our class is doing that?"

Convincing Families About the Value of Class Meetings

Most parents did not have class meetings when they were in school and may question the amount of time their children spend in meetings during that first month of school. You need to share the concepts and skills that children are learning in these meetings as they start the day with a positive tone, plan what they are going to do during the day, make joint decisions, and solve conflicts. When families realize what their children are learning in class meetings, they are generally more supportive. The following are concepts and skills that children learn in class meetings:

- listening without interrupting
- taking turns talking
- explaining something you know
- learning to weigh options
- exploring different points of view
- asking related questions
- consulting multiple resources to answer a single question
- collaborating in varied activities
- expressing an opinion or a position
- disagreeing without criticizing

- considering possible solutions to a problem
- understanding available choices
- choosing among options
- having reasons for opinions
- reaching consensus
- voting
- learning to live with the outcome of a vote
- choosing and trying out one procedure
- evaluating a process

Even skeptical parents will be impressed by the skills their young children are acquiring when presented with such a detailed list as this. This information can be shared in family letters, like the samples on page 73, or in family meetings.

Letter to Families
About Class Meetings

Dear Families:

   This year your child will participate in class meetings. Every day we will spend a few minutes talking about how we want our class to be. Some days we might talk about how to walk down the hall without disturbing other classes. Or we might discuss how to tell someone else they are being annoying without yelling "Stop!" Or we might share ideas about how to join a group of children that are playing together. If it can be a problem in our class, we'll talk about it in our class meetings.

   Rather than just getting children to follow the rules, I want them to think about how what they say and what they do affects other people. I want them to treat others well because it is the right thing to do, not just to keep from getting in trouble. So in class meetings, we will all think about how to get along with others.

   You may want to ask your child what we talked about in our class meeting each day. That way you can be a part of our class meetings.

Sincerely,

Letter to Families
About What Children Learn in Class Meetings

Dear Families:

   A few weeks ago I wrote to you about the class meetings we have every day. You would be very proud of your children if you could see how much they have learned about problem solving since school began. In addition to learning to treat each other better, they are learning other important social skills in these meetings. They are learning to listen without interrupting each other, and they are learning to take turns talking, which, as you know, is not easy for young children.

   They are also learning to express their own opinion, disagree without criticizing, and explore different points of view, all of which are very difficult for young children. These are social skills that many adults need to develop.

   Even though these children are young, they are learning very important skills that will help them get along better with their classmates in school and will serve them well as they grow up to become successful adults.

   If you can arrange your schedule to join us for a class meeting, you are welcome any day.

Sincerely,

Dealing With an Individual Child's Misbehavior

Inevitably, there are individual children who require more guidance than other children. Once again, we look on these situations as opportunities to help the misbehaving child internalize self-control. When a child engages in behavior that has been identified by the class as inappropriate, we first remind the child of the appropriate behavior. This might be as simple as saying, "Corey, I'm noticing that you are yelling when the block tower falls down. Our class agreed that there is never a time when it is okay to yell in the classroom. What other things can you do to show the fun of watching the tower fall down?" After a quick discussion of alternate ways to behave, we leave the area, suggesting to Corey that he is on his own and is responsible, once again, for his self-control.

If the misbehavior persists, then we offer the child an opportunity to choose another activity (center, area of the room in which to work, and so on) where he or she can exhibit self-control. Sometimes moving or changing activities is enough to get the child back on track. We might say, "Corey, you agreed to speak in a quiet voice. Now I hear you yelling again. Since you chose to yell, you need to choose another place to work where you can use self-control." We then help Corey choose another activity, and he begins to work with his new choice.

Finally, if the misbehavior persists in the new location, we choose an activity (center, area of the room in which to work, and so on) where we think the child can be self-controlled. We say, "Corey, you are yelling as you build with the Legos®. Yelling is not acceptable in this class. Please move to the listening center where you will not have to talk and can think about your self-control."

It is important that you deal with the child in a calm, controlled manner. Do not berate the child, listing the misbehaviors for all to hear. Instead, quietly remind the child of the chances he or she had to make good choices and how the child chose not to use self-control. During the process, watch for successful implementation of the agreed-upon behavior and reinforce that behavior. At the end of the time period, express concern to the child about

---

Teacher Tip

Three Steps to Guiding a Child's Behavior

1. Remind the child of the appropriate behavior.

2. Offer the opportunity to make another choice about the behavior (moving to a different place, changing the materials the child works with, and so on).

3. Choose a place for the child where he or she can work quietly or alone.

the behavior and offer hope for the next interaction's success. You might say "Juan, I'm sorry that you didn't get to build and knock down towers for all of center time today. But when you choose to throw blocks you are showing that you aren't using the self-control you need. Today you remembered longer than you did before and I think you'll soon be able to work for all of center time without throwing blocks."

It takes time for some children to behave in appropriate ways, but by supporting individual children you help them learn to make beneficial decisions about their behavior. Reinforcing positive behaviors in children is also beneficial to their social development.

Reinforcing Positive Behaviors

We want to reinforce children's positive behaviors. However, we do not want to resort to empty praise. Teachers sometimes fall into a habit of using certain phrases such as "I really like that," or "Good job." Repeated comments such as those quickly lose their meaning, or worse, these phrases become an adult's way of manipulating children's behavior (Kohn, 2001).

> Recognition supports learning. It leads to a sense of belonging, personal power, and an intrinsic motivation to learn.
> — *Caren Cameron, Beth Tate,*
> *Daphne MacNaughton,*
> *and Colleen Politano, 1997*

When teachers—or parents—use throw-away phrases like "Good job" too often, children begin looking to adults to evaluate the work that they do or the ways they behave toward other people. Rather than motivating children to continue working hard or acting respectfully toward others, some research shows that this kind of praise makes children less willing to work hard, less eager to help others, and only more dependent on praise. "As if it weren't bad enough that 'Good job!' can undermine independence, pleasure, and interest, it can also interfere with how good a job children actually do." (Kohn, 2001, p. 26)

This does not mean that children's hard work or empathetic gestures should go unnoticed. Children deserve recognition, but recognition in an authentic way.

Some experts contend that true recognition is:

- **authentic:** based on genuine accomplishments that occur every day

- **personal:** based on participation and choices of students

- **inclusive:** available to all students without condition

- **varied:** provides infinite opportunities for recognizing students' successes.

(Cameron, et al., 1997, p. 8)

One way to provide true recognition for children's efforts without using praise or rewards is simply to rephrase what we say to children. Instead of statements of praise, provide precise feedback that specifically describes the students' behavior or efforts. Some comments that meet all the characteristics of true recognition include:

- "I can see that you put a lot of work into this."

- "I noticed that you stopped your work to help Joshua find the marker he lost. That was very kind."

- "Sarah looked scared when she fell on the playground. You really helped her feel better by helping her stand up and walking with her to the nurse's office."

- "I saw you writing a note to Sheneka during writing workshop. Sheneka is feeling sad today, and you were trying to help her feel better. That was a thoughtful thing to do."

- "You revised that beginning three times and now you have it like you want it."

Teacher Tip

Convincing Families Not to Say "Good Job"

Weekly letters can help families understand the language encouraged in class. The letter on page 77 can help families understand some kinds of true recognition for them to use with their children.

Another form of true recognition is asking questions about how the child feels. Alfie Kohn asks us to consider this question: "Why tell him what part of his drawing impressed you when you can ask him what he likes best about it? Asking 'What was the hardest part to draw?' or 'How did you figure out how to make the feet the right size?' is likely to nourish his interest in drawing. Saying 'Good job!' as we've seen, may have exactly the opposite effect." (Kohn, 2001, p. 28)

Getting to Know Each Child

All young children have similar interests and needs; however, we recognize that each child is a unique individual. The better we get to know each child, the better we can teach them. The more we know about each child, the easier it is to support that child's development of self-control.

Teachers come to know children individually, culturally, and developmentally by taking time to observe and interact with students and by understanding the stages of child development.
— Paula Denton and Roxann Kriete, 1999

   By taking time to learn about students, to get to know them as individuals, you show that you care about children and respect them as individuals. To remind themselves of this point, some teachers post the adage "They don't care what you know until you show that you care" in a prominent place where it is visible every day.

Comments
From a First-Grade Teacher

Camilla's off-task behavior could erupt at any time. It did not take me long to notice that Camilla had a better day when I made a special effort to welcome her to the class. Her mother loved her, but did not demonstrate that caring to her. Camilla needed to know that I cared.

So, every morning, I made a point of speaking directly to Camilla. The interaction did not last long, but I conveyed the message that I cared about her and was glad she was at school that day. Sometimes we would talk about her clothes, or I'd ask about her homework—nothing profound, just a connection between us.

You need to get to know all kinds of things about the children in your classes. As a start, you need to know about:

- immediate family members,

- family values,

- extended family he or she sees often or is particularly close to,

- pets,

- interests,

- fears,

- how he or she is comforted,

- favorite activities,

- strengths, and

- areas that need to be strengthened.

One way to get to know children a bit better is to ask their families to write an introductory note to you about their child. Requesting this information in a caring, thoughtful way reassures families that you have the best interests of their child at the forefront. The sample letter on page 79 is one way to word the inquiry.

Letter to Families
at the Beginning of the Year

Dear Families:

   The more I know about your children, the better I can teach them. You know more about your child than anyone else does. You could help me be a better teacher by sharing with me some information about your child and your family.

   Would you find a few minutes to write whatever you think would help me get to know your child and your family? You may want to think about these questions: What is your child like at home? What does your child like to play with? Who are your child's friends? What does your family like to do together? Does your child have brothers and sisters? How do they get along?

   Thanks for taking the time to write.

Best regards,

The more you know about a child, the better you can identify the child's developmental levels and instructional needs, while you plan how to help move that child forward.

Comments
From a Kindergarten Teacher

It was the fifth day of school and my class was joining the huge lunch line in the cafeteria. Lunch can be a chaotic time in elementary schools until all the routines are in order, because the youngest students in the building are the ones who start the whole process.

   I noticed a little boy in the class ahead of mine throw himself on the floor. He began kicking the floor and crying as loud as he could. Other children gathered around him, just watching him. I knew this was going to slow down the line, and cut into the time that my students had to eat their lunches. This little boy's teacher was very pregnant, so I thought I would help with this situation.

Comments (continued)

I walked over to the child, knelt down, and touched him on the shoulder. I started talking in a calm, quiet voice, believing that my calm demeanor would help him find some sense of quiet. In the past, that approach had worked with dozens of children who were out of control. Not this time. The second I touched the child, he began to scream even louder and kicked harder, this time directed at me. His teacher rushed over to us, shouting, "Take your hand off of him. Don't touch him." She sat on the floor beside him and said to him very directly, "Get control. Do not kick. Do not yell. Stand up now." He did exactly as she said, which totally surprised me. The teacher and I exchanged glances and I shrugged. Both of us had too much to do getting our students through the lunch line and seated for lunch to talk at that point.

After school, she came to my room and explained that this child had been physically abused and could not tolerate anyone touching him. His foster parents had talked with her about his impulsive behavior, his inability to control his anger, and how he needed adults to talk him through his outbursts.

Asking families to write a letter about their child can help you learn many things about that child. This is usually an open-ended assignment, perhaps a paragraph added at the end of a family letter. For example, you might write, "As I get to know the children in the class, I wonder what each one is like at home. I wonder what favorite things your child likes to do, what your family does for fun, and what hopes and dreams you have for your child. Please write me a letter describing your child. It does not have to be long, but fill me in on things I need to know about your family (and the extended family as well)."

Making careful observations of children during the first weeks of school can help you get to know each child. Many early childhood educators like to note each child's personality, likes or dislikes, response to others, attitude, and disposition during the first weeks of school. They keep up with this information by making anecdotal notations on self-sticking address labels. By labeling the top of a sheet of labels as "personality," you can note clues that help you understand each child's personality. Then by looking at that label sheet, you can see at a glance which children you have not watched as closely as others. Labeling each sheet ensures

Response to Others	
Dorian	Mariel
Catherine 9-3 kind response to Terica; helped look for lost necklace	Justin
William	Shawn 9-3 argument w/ Corey about turn taking
Ashley C.	Cory 9-3 argument w/ Shawn about turn taking
Mary Beth	Ashleigh G. 9-3 always seems to say "Ty" and please
Kendall 9-4 sat with new friends in lunchroom	Nicole
Molly 9-4 worked cooperatively with William to sort books	Kim
Matt	Merillat
Marcus	Derek 9-5 unwilling to be Mary's partner in math - just wants to be w/ boys?
Mary 9-5 sat alone in lunchroom - even w/ my suggestions	Terica
King Lee	Kristofere

that every child is being observed for every trait. Forms such as the one above also record a teacher's anecdotal notations.

Many beginning-of-school activities also offer opportunities for you to get to know the children. As children share the title of their favorite book, tell their favorite "out of school" activity, or mention personal facts ("I have two dogs and one of them gets in trouble when he climbs on the dining table"), you have a unique opportunity to see a child's life through that child's eyes. By staging "getting to know you" activities, you can learn about children in the class.

It is important to reiterate that teachers have a unique position in the life of a child. The child comes to you with little or no prior knowledge about you, and you come to the child with little or no prior knowledge about him or her. Both you and the child need time at the beginning of the year to learn about each other and the other people in the class. This "learning about a new person" may be unfamiliar to children who have not been in school before or who have not had many adults, other than family, in their lives. Teachers who realize that getting to know their children is important also work hard to meet all the needs of children in the class.

Meeting Children's Needs

Just as teachers recognize appropriate behavior as a way of acknowledging children who make good decisions about the way they interact with their peers, they also monitor and try to meet each child's needs. Of course, this is not possible during the first week of school in a class of twenty or thirty children. But, after a few weeks, most teachers know their children well enough that they can identify most needs of most children. Meeting a need for a child can be as simple as offering a supporting, encouraging smile during the school day or as involved as finding appropriate social services for a family.

It is helpful to remember Maslow's Hierarchy of Needs when thinking about meeting children's needs. Maslow contended that the needs at the lowest level of his hierarchy have the most potency. The lower needs have to be met before a person is motivated to try to fulfill higher needs.

- The lowest level of Maslow's Hierarchy of Needs is the physiological needs, food and drink.

- The next level is safety—both security and psychological safety.

- The third level is belongingness and love, which includes the sense of affiliation, acceptance by others, and affection from those closest to the person.

- The fourth level is self-esteem, competence, approval, and recognition.

All of these needs must be met before a child can focus on cognitive tasks. Children are not going to be thinking about appropriate behavior if their physical needs are not met. A child who snatches a cereal box away from another child may be hungry, not malicious. Young children may attack other children—verbally or physically—when they do not feel psychologically safe in the classroom. They may attack because they feel others may attack them. A child who gets in an argument over the appearance of her clothes will not feel as if she is accepted by her peers. She may be unable to find the clean clothes at home among the dirty ones or may not have any clean clothes to wear to school. Children who have not been allowed to do things for themselves will not feel competent or feel like they have approval of others. Teachers need to meet children's physical, safety, belongingness, and esteem needs. As you get to know your students better, you'll be better able to judge how to meet the individual needs of children.

Comments
From a Kindergarten Teacher

I think of Eliza when I think about a child who needed me to meet some of her emotional needs. Her father was very exacting in everything that went on in their family, and poor Eliza did not see herself as able to do anything without an adult's help. Why should she try? Her father would redo it or tell her how to redo it. She needed help learning to do her share in the class, so I began a campaign to help Eliza feel more competent. I found special jobs around the classroom for her to do. I would say things like, "I noticed how you sorted those pattern blocks yesterday, would you help me sort the construction paper into separate colors?" And I purposefully did not tell her how to do the job. I just accepted however she did it. It was not long until she was trying things on her own, beginning to believe that she could do things on her own, and feeling better about herself as a person.

Summary

The first week of school is a very busy time for early childhood educators. As you help children learn to see each other as friends and as resources for assistance, also offer interesting, engaging learning experiences, teach more routines, and lead effective class meetings. Throughout all of this activity, you also get to know each student and begin meeting children's physical, social, and emotional needs.

CHAPTER 4

THE FIRST MONTH OF SCHOOL:
Continuing to Teach

As the first week of school passes and you move into the second, third, and fourth weeks of school, continue teaching children behaviors that you expect of them. Continue holding conversations about appropriate behavior in daily class meetings and continue teaching routines that are so important in supporting children's behavior during different times of the school day.

We constantly model for children the behavior that we want them to imitate, and use the pondering, reflecting, and wondering aloud strategies (discussed in Chapter 2) to explain our actions. We use the phrase "thinking in my brain" to remind our students what they should be thinking in their brains as they go about a task. For example, when we begin to carry out a routine that has previously been introduced but still needs reinforcement, we might say something like, "Now I need to get a new sharpened pencil because this one broke, and the teacher said that I can get one when I need one unless it is in the middle of an important meeting or something. So I checked and it is not an important meeting, so I'll go across the room to get one. I will not bother anyone along the way because my friends are working." This strategy of thinking aloud gives children another chance at internalizing a routine.

Beginning the second week of school, we expand the routines we teach students to include what we expect of them during different academic times of the day, specifically during reading, writing, and math times. During these times of the day we work with small groups, so it is important that other students know what they are expected to do and are actively engaged in those routines. As children are working independently or in small groups, we spend time monitoring how well they carry out each routine. We also pay attention to transitions between activities. Young children often need time to learn to switch from one activity to another, and we support this learning by using different transition activities.

Getting to know a group of children takes time; however, by the second or third week of school, it is usually apparent which children are going to need additional support to learn the rules and routines of the class. We think it is important to involve the families of these students early in the school year. We want families to be familiar with the ways our classes operate and how they can help support their children in this learning process. We often begin involving families by asking them to join us in a class meeting. Families are not typically aware of how class meetings are used in our classes.

Continuing Class Meetings

It is important to continue having class meetings on a regular basis. Some teachers choose to have daily meetings. Others choose to meet only once or twice a week. The frequency of class meetings depends on how well students have developed a sense of community and how many problems are occurring in the class that need to be addressed by the whole group.

> The goal of group time is not to sing the song, read the story, or do the calendar. These activities are in the service of broader, long-term goals such as the development of self-regulation, cooperation, and perspective-taking.
> — Rheta DeVries and Betty Zan, 1994

What Children Say About Class Meetings

Che: Friends can help you solve a problem.

Crissy: You don't tell on kids like at my old school. You ask the teacher for help solving a problem.

Jorge: I learn about what problems can happen between two people.

Matthew: I learn there are a lot more ways to solve problems than fighting. It gives me a chance to find out that I'm not the only one with problems.

Stacie: It gives you a chance to grow up a little. It gives you a chance to solve problems on your own instead of going to the teacher.

Checking In

During the first month of school, the focus of class meetings changes. Instead of discussing class rules or practicing class routines, some meetings focus on the question of how well the rules and routines are working. This type of class meeting is often called a *check-in meeting*.

If we notice a certain rule that is being broken by more than one child, we bring up this issue in a class meeting. We ask children to role-play the situation, dramatizing the inappropriate behavior as well as the positive way to follow a rule or guideline. During the conversation, children often remind each other why a particular rule was established. The discussion during a check-in meeting triggers children's memories about previous conversations, and usually, this translates into more appropriate behavior about the issue being discussed.

> If check-in meetings are worked into the fabric of daily or weekly classroom life, they can provide children with a sustained experience of their class as a dynamic, caring community.
> — *Child Development Project, 1996*

Contributing to the Agenda

At the beginning of the year, you might select topics for class meetings, but it does not always remain your responsibility. You should not be the only person to put an issue on the agenda for class meetings. Children need opportunities to bring up issues that they consider problems.

For children whose writing you can read, a large envelope can be posted in a prominent place in the classroom. Children write a topic on a piece of paper and put it in the Class Meeting Agenda envelope. Whoever is leading the class meeting reads each topic and asks the person who wrote the note if this issue still needs to be discussed by the whole class. Often by the time the meeting occurs, the child has solved the problem and no longer needs the group's assistance.

For children who are not yet fluent writers, you can set aside part of writing workshop—or recess or any other time during the day—to take dictation from children who want to put an issue on the class meeting agenda.

When children know they can ask the whole class for help to solve their problems, they begin to see their classmates as resources. They are more likely to ask individuals for help than they would be in classes where children were not part of putting together agendas for meetings.

Comments
From a First-Grade Teacher

I had class meetings with my classes for two years before I was willing to let children put items on the agenda. I was afraid that this would lead to a different version of tattling, that children would be constantly looking for things to write about. To be honest, it was that way for about a week after I told the children about the agenda envelope. I did not like what it seemed to be doing to relationships in the class. I thought about limiting the number of pieces of paper any one person could write. I thought about limiting the number of student issues we would deal with in any one meeting. I actually thought about taking the envelope away all together. But after some time I realized that if I believed in class meetings and children's abilities to solve problems, I needed to take the problem to them. I explained what I thought I was seeing, and expressed how

Comments (continued)

disappointed I was that so many people seemed to be having problems they could not solve on their own. Then I turned it over to the class. They talked for several minutes, then decided that there would be three guidelines, that people could write agenda items only if:

♦ the problem was really serious,

♦ the person had tried to solve it on his or her own, and

♦ the person had asked one other person to help him or her solve the problem.

That decision cut the complaints in half the next week. Within three weeks, there were very few items put on the agenda by children. They went back to solving most problems on their own, and only asked for help when they really needed it.

Learning Academic Routines

Just as logistical routines help the class run more smoothly, academic routines also help those instructional times of the day operate equally smoothly. Instructional times are more effective when children clearly understand what is expected of them during that time. When academic routines are carefully explained to children and practiced many times, most children internalize what is expected of them. They follow the routines and lapse into fewer behavioral problems that distract from learning.

Since we believe that teaching children routines is better than repeatedly reminding them of what they should be doing, we present academic routines in the same way we described in Chapter 3 about presenting logistical or behavioral routines. We teach a few routines at a time and practice them until most of the children are following each routine without prompting. Then we use questioning techniques instead of continuing to tell children what to do. That is, rather than telling off-task children what they should be doing, we ask children, "What should you be doing now?" Most of the time, this simple question is enough to redirect children's actions back to the more appropriate behavior of one of the academic routines.

In other early childhood classrooms, many behavior problems happen during times when children do not know what to do—or when children have to wait several minutes for the teacher to give instructions. Creating academic routines for various subject areas that address these lost snippets of time can prevent many behavior problems.

Reading Routines

Reading instruction is more effective when teachers work with small groups of children instead of the whole class. Time with a small group is most effective when other children in the class are involved in an engaging activity. Interrupting the work of a small group of children to redirect the behavior of children outside the group is annoying. But more than that, those kinds of interruptions take away from the learning of children in the small group. Teaching specific routines is an effective way to get children independently involved in quality experiences where they learn important reading concepts and skills while you work with a small group.

As in working through logistical routines, academic routines need to be discussed with children in detail and practiced many times before they can be expected to go through a routine on their own. The reading routines you teach children depend on the concepts and skills they need to be learning. A few reading routines are described in the box on page 90–91.

Teacher Tip

Routines Require Practice

Children need time to learn a routine. Teach only one or two routines in a day. Practice those routines two or three times on the day taught, and two or three times a day for several more days until children appear to internalize the routines.

Children learning to read are active agents, initiating and assuming responsibility for their learning.
— *Sharon Taberski, 2000*

Reading Routines

Reading the Room: Find a partner. Decide who will go first. Together get the pointer. One child holds the pointer, points to a word or a phrase, and reads it to the partner. The partner listens carefully, making sure that the child is reading correctly, and follows the child around the room. The first child continues pointing and reading words until the partners come back to the place in the room where they started. Then the partners switch roles. When finished, return the pointer to the place where it belongs.

Partner Reading: Find a partner who agrees to be a serious reader and a respectful listener. Choose a book to read to each other. Together find a quiet place in the room and take turns reading. When finished, return the books to the containers in the reading center where they belong.

Newspaper Words: Find a newspaper page and a highlighter. Choose one letter of the alphabet (or words from the word wall). Highlight that letter (or word) as many times as it can be found. When finished, write your name on the top of the newspaper page, put it in the work basket, and return the highlighter to the container in the writing center where it belongs.

Making Magnetic Word Wall Words: Find a baking tray and a container of magnetic letters. Take these and find a place on the floor near the word wall. Put the letters on the floor faceup. Choose one word from the word wall and find all the letters that make that word. Keep choosing words and spelling them with magnetic letters. When finished, put all letters back in the container. Return the tray and the container of letters to the places where they belong.

Poetry Reading: Find a partner who agrees to be a serious reader, and together select a poetry folder from the reading center. Together choose five favorite poems and choral-read those poems. When finished, return the poetry folder to the place in the reading center where it belongs.

Graphic Organizers: Working with a partner, choose one graphic organizer for stories. Talk about the parts of the story that the chart asks about. Use dry-erase pens to complete the chart. When finished, put the graphic organizer in the storage basket in the writing center, and return the pen to the place in the writing center where it belongs.

Retellings: Find the handheld recorder in the listening center and take it to a quiet place in the classroom. Decide which story to tell. Push the record button. Say your name, the date, and the title of the story. Then tell the story. When finished, say, "The End" and push the stop button. Return the recorder to its place in the listening center.

Comments
From a First-Grade Teacher

For a long time I was convinced that there would be chaos in the room if I allowed six-year-olds to make decisions about what they would do during reading time. Reading conferences were important to me, and I was convinced that they were wonderful for children to support them as beginning readers. But I was afraid that the children I was not working with would interrupt a dozen times if they were working on self-selected activities. I was a worksheet hold-out because I knew those worksheets kept children busy on their own work without bothering me.

Finally, last year I gave in and decided to try it. Everyone else on my grade-level team had child-selected activities during reading workshop. After two weeks, I knew that I had been wrong. My colleagues had been right. Children were much more engaged in the reading activities that they chose than they ever were with the worksheets.

Families often feel most comfortable supporting their child's reading at home. They realize that learning to read takes a lot of time in early childhood classes and that their child needs support at home. However, they do not always understand what goes on during "reading class" at school. A family letter, such as the one below, can help families understand how to best support their child.

Letter to Families
About Reading Routines

Dear Families:

This week the class learned two reading routines. I thought you might like to know these and practice them at home when you have time. The children learned—and practiced—Partner Reading and Making Magnetic Word Wall Words. Your child can probably explain the routines to you, but just in case, I'll describe them for you.

Partner Reading: Find a partner who agrees to be a serious reader and a respectful listener. Choose a book to read to each other. Together find a quiet place in the room and take turns reading. When finished, return the books to the containers in the reading center where they belong.

Making Magnetic Word Wall Words: Find a baking tray and a container of magnetic letters. Take these and find a place on the floor near the word wall. Put the letters on the floor faceup. Choose one word from the word wall and find all the letters that make that word. Keep choosing words and spelling them with magnetic letters. When finished, put all letters back in the container. Return the tray and the container of letters to the places where they belong.

You can do partner reading with any books you have at home. Your child can tell you some of our word-wall words. They are simple words that the children are learning to read without sounding out. Some of these words are: *at, am, to, it, is, was, the,* and *and*.

Sincerely,

Writing Routines

If children learn to write by writing, as Donald Graves contends, you have to create an environment where writing is the class's focus for a period of time. Without routines, writing time can be chaotic. Like any other time in an early childhood classroom, chaos easily leads to less than appropriate behavior.

Most writing workshops follow the format below:

- mini-lesson

- status of the class

- writing time/conferences

- sharing time

Children need to be taught exactly how they are to leave the group; where to retrieve their writing folder, paper, and a writing utensil; and where they may sit to write. At the end of the class's writing time, children need to know who is going to share that day and what they are expected to do with their writing folder if they are sharing (or not sharing). Several writing routines are described in the box on page 94.

…writing is something important that takes time to learn…people learn to write by writing…if practice doesn't make perfect, it at least makes progress.
— *Donald Graves, 1983*

Writing Routines

Getting Started: After you respond to the status of the class, go directly to the writing folder box. Find your writing folder. Put one hand on each side of the writing folder, holding it so papers do not fall out. Walk to the writing center and select paper. Stamp the date on that paper. Choose a pencil or markers. Find a quiet place in the room and begin writing.

Getting Response From a Partner: When you reach the point when you need a response from another person, choose one person who will be a serious response partner. Walk quietly to where that person is working and ask if he or she has time to listen to a piece of writing. Together find a quiet place in the classroom. Ask for revision or editing help, then read the paper so that the person can hear it easily.

Getting Response From a Group: When you reach the point when you need a response and you want a response from more than one person, choose people who will be serious response partners. Walk quietly to where those people are working and ask if they have time to listen to a piece of writing. Ask them to meet you in a quiet place in the classroom. Ask for revision or editing help, then read the paper so the group can hear it easily.

Pair–Share: Everyone brings one piece of writing to the group meeting area and sits in a circle. Everyone turns their bodies so they are facing a partner. Taking turns, they read what they wrote that day. After the first reading the other person makes at least one positive comment about the writing and asks one question to help that person make his or her writing better.

Reading Your Writing to the Whole Group: Sit in the Author's Chair. Put your legs out straight or cross them on the chair. Put your arms at your sides and hold the paper with both hands. Read so that your voice is loud enough for everyone to hear. Read with expression so the audience will be interested. When finished, call on other students for comments, questions, or connections.

Putting Writing Away if You Are Sharing That Day: Put all your papers, except the one you are sharing, back into your writing folder. Make sure no papers stick out from the folder. Put all pencils and markers back where they belong. Leave your writing folder where you are writing. Go to the meeting area with only the piece of writing you are going to read to the group.

Putting Writing Away if You Are Not Sharing That Day: Put all papers back into the writing folder. Make sure no papers are sticking out from the folder. Put all pencils and markers back where they belong. Put your writing folder back in the writing-folder container. Go to the meeting area, sit quietly, and get ready to listen to other people's work.

Often families do not know how to support their child's writing development. They are unsure of what to say when their child asks how to spell a word, and may concentrate on the mechanics of writing before their child even records initial sounds. Family letters, like the sample below, keep parents informed and make suggestions about procedures to implement at home to support their child's writing development.

Letter to Families
About Writing Routines

Dear Families:

Every day after the class has spent some time writing, some children read what they've written to the whole class. We have a list of which children read aloud on which day. That is why your child may have told you that he or she is a "Monday reader" or a "Thursday reader."

I do not force a child to read if he or she does not want to, but most children want to read their writing to the class. But as you can imagine, young children are not always the best readers in front of the group. They often hold the paper in front of their faces so it is hard to hear them. They often read in very quiet voices.

Today we talked about reading aloud to the class and came up with a new reading routine. We agreed to do these things when reading to the whole group:

> Sit in the Author's Chair. Put your legs out straight or cross them on the chair. Put your arms at your sides and hold the paper with both hands. Read so that your voice is loud enough for everyone to hear. Read with expression so the audience will be interested. When finished, call on other students for comments, questions, or connections.

You may want to practice this routine with your child at home.

Sincerely,

Math Routines

Math time in early childhood classrooms often involves working with manipulatives. While you might introduce some manipulatives during the first week, most are gradually introduced during the first month of school. When young children first use manipulatives, this can become a chaotic time unless they know how to procure them, how to work with them in a safe, organized way, and how to put them back where they belong when math time is over. Children learn these things when teachers are explicit about what they expect during math time. Wise early childhood educators explain their expectations to young children as routines.

There are decisions about some math routines that the class needs to make together. For example, if children know the routine of cupping their hands over the dice and gently shaking two times before cracking open the bottom part of their hands so the dice can gently fall to the game board, working with dice goes much more smoothly. Children do not have to crawl around the room to chase flying dice, and dice are not as easily lost.

Other procedural routines must be established, such as who goes first and second, what to do when the spinner lands on the line, what if there is a tie, what if the cards do not come out even, and so on. Each of these questions has an easy answer—it does not really matter if the spinner is spun again or if the person who spun decides if it is on the right space or left.

Mathematical ideas help children understand and connect the skills they develop. When that happens, children are more likely to remember the skills and apply them when they are needed.
— *Linda Schulman Dacey and Rebeka Eston, 1999*

What is important is that the math learning time is not spent arguing over rules. When working with a partner or small group, children must decide who is first, then decide if the turns proceed in a clockwise or counter-clockwise manner. Young children often want to zigzag first, second, third, and so on across the circle. This becomes too confusing and leads to someone missing a turn, thus arguing about procedures instead of learning math. Many activities for small groups do not require enough materials for everyone to have a responsibility to procure and return the materials. A procedure must be in place to answer this question as well. In most math games, the emphasis is not on winning but on learning the skill—all children who are playing can have fun without one winning at the expense of the others.

Math Routines

Following the Teacher's Model: Demonstrating the desired behavior is the simplest way to introduce a routine. If children are asked to use pattern blocks to create a shape, then retrieve the tub of pattern blocks from the math shelf, carry it to the designated area on the floor, open the tub, and begin to select the desired blocks. While you model this behavior, verbally point out the way you carry the tub with two hands so it does not spill or how you put the lid under the box so it does not get stepped on.

Playing a Game With a Partner: Meet your partner to decide about the ground rules and who will get the supplies. Sit on the floor so both partners can face the math board. The first person goes first, and the second person watches the first person. Then the second person has a turn while the first person watches. Both people are responsible for learning the math.

Playing a Game With a Small Group: Determine the ground rules unique to the particular game you are playing. Decide how play will proceed. While the first person is playing, the other people must watch the moves, checking to see if they are correct. All players are responsible for the math learning of the game.

Writing on Dry-Erase Boards: We like to use dry-erase boards (or small chalkboards) so everyone has a place to write. If children sit in a circle, we can scan the circle quickly to see who needs help with a particular skill. Distributing the boards and markers is the most confusing thing about using dry-erase boards. Ask children to sit in a circle, then place small stacks of boards across the diameter of the circle. Children can reach for a board near them, thus avoiding having to rush to grab a board from a central location. Store the markers in two plastic cups. Pass each cup around the circle, asking each child to take a marker as the cup comes by. Place the cups in the middle of the circle until it is cleanup time, and then pass them back around the circle to collect the markers. Place a couple of tissue boxes near the stacks of boards so each child can reach for a tissue to erase the board. These same procedures work for passing out chalk and erasers for chalkboard use.

Families may not understand how playing math games supports mathematics instruction. So family letters play an important part in explaining how families can best support their children. By explaining simple concepts first, such as the procedure for partner games, families as well as their children will have a basis on which to build the more complex ideas of mathematics. The sample letter below is an example of an early family letter about mathematics.

Letter to Families
About Math Routines

Dear Families:

This week we started to play math games with partners. You know that we develop routines for many of the things we do in class. So, this week we worked out a routine for playing games with one other person. The routine is:

Meet your partner to decide about the ground rules and who will get the supplies. Sit on the floor so both partners can face the math board. The first person goes first, and the second person watches the first person. Then the second person has a turn while the first person watches. Both people are responsible for learning the math.

You may want to ask your child to teach you one of the math games we are playing and practice the "Playing a Game With a Partner" routine at home. Of course, when your child has an adult as a partner, his or her learning is extended. Ask your child questions that extend and enrich the math experience, such as:

- How do you know that I have more than you do?
- How many more?
- What is your strategy for finding the answer?
- Say your thinking out loud to me.

By talking to your child about his or her learning, you can correct misconceptions before they become habits and nudge your child on to the next concept as well.

Sincerely,

Monitoring

Even when students learn academic routines, there are times when misbehavior occurs. Students may act inappropriately when the work is too hard or too easy for them, if they do not understand the work, or cannot get help when they need it. You can avoid minor classroom disruptions by:

- scanning the class frequently to notice and respond to potential problems. Sometimes you can prevent a problem from occurring simply by walking over and standing near students who seem to be having difficulty being self-controlled. Proximity to the teacher encourages most students to choose more appropriate behavior.

- reacting calmly and quickly to a student's disruptive behavior. When you keep your voice at a quiet level, calmly stating the facts, you model behaviors of self-control for the children. "When you are in control, I can talk to you," or "I cannot understand your crying-talking, so when you get control, I can talk to you" are typical responses.

- reminding the student(s) of the classroom rule or procedure that they are not following. "Brian, our class agreed that we would… You are… How can you change your behavior to follow our agreement?" is a way of calmly responding to the situation.

- using logical consequences if necessary. For example, if a child throws the playground ball on the roof, then that child has to ask the custodian to get the ball down. Or, if a child throws the blocks from the block center, she has to choose a center that does not have anything to throw in it. The old adage "make the punishment fit the crime" is so true in these situations. If a child cannot handle a particular behavior, then that child does not have the privilege of participating in that activity.

♦ making sure other students in the class are engaged in their work, then talking quietly with the disruptive student(s). Although it may appear that the misbehaving child is "getting away with something," this is far from the truth. If the other children are engaged in their work, you have a longer period of time to talk with the child, wait for a response, and negotiate acceptable behaviors.

Dealing With Transitions

Routines make the day run more smoothly, but you also need to pay attention to the transitions between activities or learning experiences. In some early childhood classes, it takes as much as ten minutes to get children to stop one activity and refocus their attention on the next activity. This is usually because the teacher has not planned well for the transition.

It is not easy for young children to stop what they are doing and start a new activity. Many teachers give their classes what they refer to as a "five-minute warning" before children are expected to end an activity. It takes only a few seconds to give this verbal cue that it is almost time to end whatever children are working on.

At the beginning of the year, it is often easier to have every activity end with children returning to the group area. This is not something we discuss with children, but rather something that we just ask them to do. How to respond when the teacher says, "Meet me on the carpet" is one of the first transitions we teach. Even though we are asking children to come to the carpet, we might begin singing a song or reciting a poem as everyone starts walking in that direction.

Chanting a poem or singing a song can be an effective transition activity. It is best to teach these poems and songs during a large-group time. During the first month of school, we often teach two or three songs or poems each week. Not only do they become a part of the class's rituals, but the transitions are most effective when children have them memorized.

Comments
From a First-Grade Teacher

During my first year of teaching, the veteran teacher told me to sing some songs to help keep children's attention. I could not think of any songs, and then I remembered the songs we used to sing at Girl Scout camp, like "Bingo" and "John Jacob Jingleheimer Schmidt." I found my old songbook and was in business.

Talking With Families

By the second or third week of school, children are beginning to return to their normal behavior. The beginning-of-school awe has worn off. At the start of the school year, some children are more quiet than normal. Some are more boisterous than normal. By this time you have gotten to know your students fairly well and can identify the children whose behavior needs extra attention.

It is important to contact families at this time. Parents and teachers need to work together to help

children learn the behaviors that are appropriate for school. In general, parents want their child to behave at school and are willing to do what they can to help.

We begin to establish a relationship with each family as early as we can. This can be as simple as chatting with parents who pick up their child after school or calling them on the phone to share a funny anecdote from the day. We make it a point to share a positive story with each family during the first or second week of school.

We always hold a family meeting early in the year—during the first or second week of school. It is more than just meet-the-teacher night. We share lots of information about what we expect of children, what children—and their families—can expect of us, and how we guide children's behavior. We also share information about ourselves so families can see us as real people, not just "the teacher." Then we have an informal time of just chatting. This gives parents a chance to get to know us and gives us a chance to get to know the parents.

Getting to know families at the very beginning of the year and having a positive conversation with each family help to establish positive relationships between the home and school. Then when we have to contact a family to discuss a problem, it is a little easier.

Sending an informal, brief note to the family to request a conference is often better than calling them on the telephone. This gives the family a little time to reflect on the request and think about their answer. We usually handwrite these requests on informal note paper. We do not want the family to think of this as a formal complaint against their child, just the collaboration between the teacher and family who both care about the child. The request should be stated positively and outline exactly what kind of help you are seeking. Families appreciate being contacted before the problem gets out of hand and usually cooperate fully.

Talking with any family about a misbehaving child can be difficult. Parents can be intimidated by having to talk to the teacher about their child. To encourage dialogue, rather than confrontation, we offer a comfortable spot to sit where both

> September 9
>
> Dear Sherry,
>
> Do you have a few minutes to talk with me about Michael? I told you early in the year that I would let you know when I thought we needed to talk. It is not serious at the moment, but I believe in talking before the problem increases. Michael seems to get his feelings hurt whenever he is not chosen first for an activity. He cries but quickly gets over it. It would help me to know how he behaves in other situations similar to this so I know how to best support him.
>
> I am free for conferences at 1:15 each afternoon or we could talk on the phone. I'm looking forward to hearing from you.
>
> Thanks,

the family member and teacher are on the same level. We try to put the family at ease, sometimes offering a soft drink. In leading the discussion about the child we find it helps to follow these three steps:

1. State the problem.

2. Ask if the behavior is observed in other situations.

3. Reach an agreement about how to handle the problem at school.

Speaking calmly, we state the observed behaviors without accusations or inferences to explain the behavior. For example, we might say, "Something happened today that I want to talk with you about. When it was time to choose a learning center to work in, Michael wanted to go to the block center. Two other children had already chosen that center so it was not available to him. He had difficulty accepting this and began to rock back and forth, kicking his feet on the floor, screaming progressively louder. He was saying, 'But I want to go to the block center. If I can't go to the block center, I'm going to…'" The family usually inquires about our response, and we answer matter-of-factly, saying something like, "I spoke to the other children about ignoring Michael until he had his self-control back and we simply ignored his behavior. I repeated to him several times, 'When you have your self-control, come talk to me.'"

Then we inquire about how the child behaves in similar situations, saying, "I was not sure if this is a typical response and wondered how Michael usually responds when he doesn't immediately get his way." In Michael's case his parents replied that since he was their only child, there were not many times that he did not get his way. They said that he often screamed like this and when he did, they just let him have his way because they did not know what to do about the screaming.

In order to reach an agreement with the family about what interventions should be tried at school, we keep the conversation focused on the matter at hand. In this case it was obvious that the parents needed help with their parenting skills, and this turned out to be only the tip of the iceberg regarding Michael's problems. But the immediate need was for Michael to stop screaming when he did not get his way. The family agreed that ignoring the behavior and isolating him from the rest of the children was the best thing to do.

The family member you are talking to is sometimes shocked by this first contact. They may respond by denial or accusing another child or you of doing something to provoke the misbehavior. We say something like, "I'm seeking your help in getting at the root of the problem. Is there any insight you can give me to help us figure this out?" or "I understand your concerns. I'm dealing with the other child also. But I'm concerned right now about how to best help Ralph."

Comments
From a Family

Robert is our fourth child, so we have dealt with lots of teachers before. With the other children our first contact with teachers was usually a phone call saying, "We've got a problem. When can you come in for a conference?" When Robert's kindergarten teacher called the first week of school, my first thought was, "Here we go again." Imagine my surprise when Mrs. Hernandez proceeded to tell me about a child who had fallen on the playground and how Robert helped the child stand up and walk over to her. She was calling to tell me something Robert had done that was good. I told all my friends about that phone call.

During the first month of school, getting to know the families of children helps you better understand the child. Enlisting a family's help and advice creates a powerful partnership where all parties benefit.

Summary

Beginning the second week of school, continue working with children in ways that support appropriate behaviors. Conversations about rules and routines continue to shape how children behave, and you can begin introducing academic routines. As you work with children, carefully monitor their activities and provide transitions between activities. As you get to know children better, you begin to identify children who need extra support in learning appropriate school behavior and contact those families so that both home and school are working in partnership to support those children.

CHAPTER 5

THROUGHOUT THE YEAR:
Supporting Children's Behavior

The time you spend focusing on children's behavior during the first month of school is time well spent. Throughout the rest of the school year, there will be fewer behavioral problems in the class because of the time spent early on learning and practicing routines and talking about appropriate behavior during class meetings. Over time children will develop more self-control and treat each other more respectfully.

This is not to say that there will never be behavior problems among students. Any time there is a group of people who spend several hours a day in the same room, there will be interpersonal issues. This is no different because the people are young. There will be differences of opinion, disagreements, even arguments. There will be days when everyone seems out of sorts, even you. And there will be some children who seem to forget the rules or guidelines more than others.

Throughout the year there are different ways to support appropriate behavior: by continuing class meetings, using children's literature to introduce topics that affect friendships, having conversations with individual children who are having particular problems to help them set and meet behavior goals, as well as holding children accountable for their behavior.

Continuing Morning Greetings

Just as you made sure to greet all children on the first day of school, continue this morning greeting ritual throughout the school year. Position yourself near the classroom door, either standing or sitting, but in an obvious place so that children see you each time they walk into the room. Every day greet every child individually, saying something specific to that child. On some days you might only say, "Good morning, Dontelle," but on most days, make a comment that communicates to the child that you value him or her: "Hello, Christy! How is your new puppy doing?" or "Good morning, Antonio. Your skinned arm looks better. How is it feeling?" communicates to the child that you remember or notice something unique and personal about only that child. This extends the affirmation that you value the child.

You might also choose this time to remind a child of a behavior agreement made the previous day, such as "Good morning, Palmer. When you get your things put away, let's talk about the agreements we made yesterday." This serves as a reminder to the child and gets the day started with a positive reminder, instead of waiting for Palmer's behavior to be out of control to remind him of his previous agreement.

Continuing Class Meetings

Daily class meetings remain an integral part of supporting children's appropriate behavior throughout the school year. Class meetings become the central structure to the way the class is run. Hold class meetings to address behavior issues, plan for the day's learning, share achievements, or work out problems.

> When students learn to understand and respect differences, they will find it easier to have meaningful communication with others.
> — *Jane Nelsen, Lynn Lott, and H. Stephen Glenn, 2000*

When class meetings are used for many different purposes, you may have to announce the purpose for the day's meeting and sometimes even remind children about the meeting's format. As more topics are brought up in meetings, there are going to be more obvious differences in children's feelings and their thinking about issues. You will need to help children understand that these differences are normal, that an opinion different from their own is not wrong. It is just different. At these times, words—and their processes—such as *compromise*, *give-and-take*, and *negotiation* should be introduced and explained.

Comments
From a Family

At one of her family meetings, Charlotte explained how she uses class meetings. She also suggested that family meetings could become a part of the way our family solves problems and makes decisions. I didn't get a chance to suggest starting this before my child brought it up. He wanted to go swimming on Saturday but I said that we couldn't do that because we were busy. He said, "Could we have a meeting about this? Because I'd like to tell Daddy and Michelle about my ideas. My ideas are good and you should listen to me, like my teacher and my friends do in our meetings at school." Needless to say, that started us on holding family meetings. We have them regularly now and it has helped us.

Using Children's Literature to Introduce Topics That Affect Friendships

Sometimes early childhood educators use children's literature to introduce topics that need to be discussed in class meetings. Using books to help people solve problems is referred to as *bibliotherapy* (Aiex, 1993). Experts in bibliotherapy (Pardeck, 1990) believe that the group approach "...can create a feeling of belonging and can also provide security for individuals who might feel uncomfortable in situations where they are singled out for special attention. Working in a group may lead an individual to develop a different perspective and a new understanding of the problems of others." (Aiex, 1993, p. 2) This approach to problem solving fits well with the class meeting approach to problem solving and adds a richness to the classroom.

Aiex (1993) contends that there are at least nine reasons to use bibliotherapy with children:

1. to develop an individual's self-concept;

2. to increase an individual's understanding of human behavior or motivations;

3. to foster an individual's honest self-appraisal;

4. to provide a way for a person to find interest outside of self;

5. to relieve emotional or mental pressure;

6. to show an individual that he or she is not the first or only person to encounter such a problem;

7. to show an individual that there is more than one solution to a problem;

8. to help a person discuss a problem more freely; and

9. to help an individual plan a constructive course of action to solve a problem (p. 2).

Any of these reasons might be the basis for a class meeting, and there are many excellent children's books with themes that support these issues. See below for a list of books that introduce issues of exclusion, hurt feelings, stereotypes, and self-esteem.

Children's Books That Introduce Issues for Class Meeting Discussions

Amazing Grace by Mary Hoffman (Scott Foresman, 1991)

Grace loves stories and acting. Her class decides to do the play *Peter Pan*, and Grace wants to play Peter. Other children in the class insist that she cannot be Peter because he is not a girl and he is not African American. Inspired by a ballerina from Trinidad, Grace tries out for the part of Peter and is chosen. Children do not think that Grace "fits" the part of Peter merely because of what she looks like. This is a good book to introduce the idea of stereotyping and how it affects the way children treat other people.

Angel Child, Dragon Child by Michelle Maria Surat (Scholastic, 1989)

Ut's family moves from Vietnam to the United States. At school Ut's classmates do not accept her because she looks different from them and dresses differently. Not only does Ut have to deal with the rejection of her peers, but her mother is still in Vietnam and Ut misses her desperately. Eventually, children in the school come to see more similarities than differences between themselves and Ut, and begin to save money to send for Ut's mother. This book also raises issues about stereotyping and how it makes people feel. It also supports conversations about "we are all in this together," and how good it feels to help other people.

(continued)

Chrysanthemum by Kevin Henkes (Greenwillow, 1991)

Until Chrysanthemum started kindergarten, she believed her parents when they told her that her name was perfect. On the first day of school, children in her class giggle when they learn her name. A particularly mean-spirited girl, Victoria, announces that Chrysanthemum's name takes up 13 letters, and declares, "That's exactly half the letters there are in the entire alphabet!" On the second day of school, the girls join in playground threats to "pluck" Chrysanthemum and "smell her." Chrysanthemum's music teacher—whose first name is Delphinium—and her loving parents help Chrysanthemum learn to confront the taunting and to love her name again. This book is excellent to introduce a conversation about taunting and name-calling.

Crow Boy by Taro Yashima (Viking, 1995)

Crow Boy is singled out because he is different from the other children at the school. He is smaller than anyone and the other children call him *stupid* and *slowpoke*. But after six years of school, a kind teacher recognizes and nurtures Crow Boy's knowledge of birds and nature. This recognition changes everyone's ideas about Crow Boy. A class discussion about why everyone changed the way they thought about Crow Boy can easily lead into a conversation about looking for strengths in everyone.

Hooway for Wodney Wat by Helen Lester (Houghton Mifflin, 1999)

This book addresses the issues of making fun of a child with a disability—in this case, a speech impediment—and boasting and bullying. Since Wodney cannot pronounce the letter *R*, his classmates make jokes about it and often tease Wodney. However, his friends see Wodney in a whole new light when he gets rid of Camilla Capybara, the new girl who is smarter, meaner, and bigger than anyone. Camilla exactly follows Wodney's Simon Says directions. When Wodney says, "Weed the sign," only Camilla starts to pull weeds, and when he says, "Go west," the rodents collapse in a heap for a rest, but Camilla begins walking west to leave forever. Wodney has saved the day! Wodney's story can open a discussion about bullying and making fun of other children.

I Am Me by Karla Kuskin (Simon & Schuster, 2000)

A little girl insists that she is herself despite everyone telling her that she has her mother's eyes, her father's hair, and so on. While this is a short book, it provides an interesting introduction for a discussion about the uniqueness of each person.

(continued)

Jamaica Tag-Along by Juanita Havill (Houghton Mifflin, 1989)

An African-American girl, Jamaica, realizes that she is doing the exact same thing to a younger boy in the neighborhood that her brother has done to her, saying, "You can't play with me." Jamaica's older brother, Ossie, would not let her play ball with him and his friend Buzz. Later when she is building a sand castle, a little boy asks to build with her. She refuses until she realizes what she is doing. The story line in this book can open discussions about how it feels when someone else does or says something that hurts a child's feelings, and how easy it is to do to others what we dislike being done to us.

Oliver Button Is a Sissy by Tomie dePaola (Voyager Books, 1980)

Oliver Button doesn't like to do the things that most boys do. He likes to read, draw, jump rope, play with paper dolls, dress up in costumes, and dance. Boys at school call him a sissy and go so far as to paint "Oliver Button is a sissy" on a wall at school. When Oliver gives an outstanding performance at a school talent show, other children celebrate his talent and change one word on the sign they painted so that it reads, "Oliver Button is a star." What happens to Oliver Button is a good way to begin discussions about people who are different from other children in the class and how they are treated.

William's Doll by Charlotte Zolotow (HarperTrophy, 1972)

William wants a doll. His brother, the boy next door, and his father try to redirect his attention to basketball and an electric train. While he likes to play with those things, he still wants a doll. His grandmother intercedes on his behalf with wise words for his father. This book can be used to introduce a conversation about stereotyping boys and girls.

Yoko by Rosemary Wells (Hyperion, 1998)

Other children make fun of Yoko when she brings her traditional Japanese lunch, *sushi*—rice rolls with cucumber, shrimp, seaweed, and tuna—to school. Realizing Yoko's predicament, Mrs. Jenkins, the teacher, plans International Food Day. Yoko's troubles don't end easily. Timothy, her new friend, eases her rejection into acceptance by the other children. This is a good book to help children talk about what it feels like when people make fun of them.

Comments
From a Kindergarten Teacher

One morning Robert came to class late. His mother explained that a close friend of the family had died, and that they had just come from the funeral home. Robert was obviously upset. He walked to a private place in the room and just sat alone. When I asked, he told me that he wanted to do nothing. At our next class meeting, I explained to the class that Robert was very sad because a good friend had died.

Without a word to me, one of the students left the meeting area and started looking through a basket of books. She pulled out a copy of *Nana Upstairs & Nana Downstairs* by Tomie dePaola and took it to Robert's private place. She sat down beside him, commented that this book might make him feel better, and began to read the book (using the illustrations to drive the story she told).

I was more than touched. Here was a five-year-old using a book to help another five-year-old deal with grief. I think that would have happened only in a class where children had learned to value each other and value books.

It is important to continue to keep families informed about the class's activities regarding behavior issues. When families know what books you are reading or what language you are using, they can support that at home. A sample family letter that addresses this is in on page 113.

Letter to Families
About Name-Calling

Dear Families:

One of the issues that has come up in the class is name-calling. What started as innocent fun has hurt some children's feelings. To address this problem and have a class meeting about it, I began by reading Kevin Henkes's book *Chrysanthemum* (Greenwillow, 1991).

In this book Chrysanthemum thinks that her name is perfect—until she starts kindergarten. Some children giggle when they hear her name and one girl meanly announces that, "Chrysanthemum's name has exactly half the letters there are in the entire alphabet!" The name-calling continues until the music teacher befriends Chrysanthemum.

After discussing the book, the children seemed to understand how innocent name-calling can hurt other children's feelings. The class agreed to call people by their right names and to be careful about hurt feelings. Please let me know if your child expresses any concerns about this.

Best regards,

Having Conversations With Individual Children

Some young children have more difficulty than others in maintaining self-control. Some cannot remember what is expected of them. Others can articulate rules or guidelines, but have trouble using them to adjust their own behavior. Other children have every intention of following class rules, but are so impulsive that they act before they think. Some behaviors are very ingrained in children. If children have grown up in situations where they learned to get what they want by hitting—or crying, whining, pouting, and so on—using words will not be an easy thing for them to do.

Appropriate classroom behavior will not be learned overnight. Changes in behavior are not easy and inevitably take time. Each child understands and begins to practice appropriate

> **The teacher must recognize the difficult child's underlying need to connect and bond with others and potential ability to resolve problems.**
> — *Rheta DeVries and Betty Zan, 1994*

We help students maintain accountability and integrity when they are involved in the creation and choosing of solutions.
— *Jane Nelsen, Lynn Lott, and H. Stephen Glenn, 2000*

behavior at a different time. So then the issue becomes what to do when rules are broken or guidelines are forgotten.

We believe that punishment for breaking or forgetting rules does not really help a child remember the more appropriate behaviors that we are trying to encourage. We view the times when a child behaves inappropriately as a teaching opportunity, similar to the teachable moments we take advantage of during reading workshops or math times. Sometimes reminding a child of the appropriate behavior or asking questions about what "should have been done" gets old for the adult, but children need time and reminders to change behaviors.

We find that a four-step approach works best in talking with individual children about misbehavior:

1. Move near the child. Your proximity offers the child support and gives a sense of privacy to the conversation.

2. Call attention to the problem at hand. Without this step, the child may not understand which behavior you are talking about. This is as simple as quietly saying, "Tommy, please check yourself and see what your hands are doing," or "I hear a lot of noise coming from your area."

3. After the inappropriate behavior stops, remind the child of the established expectation or ask a question that leads the child to think about what should have been done instead of what occurred. For example, "What were you supposed to be doing during this time?" or "What could you have done instead?"

4. After the inappropriate behavior is identified and the appropriate behavior is discussed, obtain a commitment from the child to try again. Inquiring of the child, "Can you agree to…now?" or "Are you ready to… now?" places the control of the situation back with the child, and supports the child as you offer another chance.

Teachers' Language That Supports Guidance Conversations

Language for Calling Attention to Misbehaviors

"I am noticing that you are…"

"I see you are getting out of control about…"

"It seems you are…"

"Your mouth (hands, feet, and so on) is doing the wrong thing."

"I see you have written only two lines on your paper. Your…is interfering with your work."

Language for Inquiring About Expectations

"Our class agreed that we would… How are you keeping up with that agreement?"

"Was there something going on that caused you to…?"

"I am going to help you with your self-control."

"Read the part that tells what our agreement is about…"

"Is this a happy face or sad face behavior?"

> **Language for Obtaining a Commitment to Try Again**
>
> "Do you want me to give you a signal?"
>
> "I know you…at home, but at school we… Can you agree to…?"
>
> "You behave more nicely than that. How can this be changed?"
>
> "You make better choices than this. Can you agree to…?"
>
> "What can I do to help you remember?"
>
> "How can we solve this?"

Before you formally address the child, you may give nonverbal cues to him as well. Sometimes making personal contact to show the child that you are aware of the misbehavior is enough to redirect his behavior. If you are already in close proximity to the child, you might touch his leg or ruffle his hair. If you are not close to the child, you might catch his eye and give a slight shake of the head, raise an eyebrow, or shrug your shoulders with a questioning look on your face. Holding your hands with the palms facing up and using a grimace to indicate that you are questioning the observed behavior is an effective technique. That gesture asks, "What is going on?" without using words.

Additionally, depending on the child and the particular situation, you may offer some generic verbal reminders about behavior. Comments such as, "Chelsea, you knew that I touched you on the knee. What was I saying to you when I did that?" or "When I…that means for you to check your behavior," or even the simple "Well, I am here. What is next?" can redirect a child's behavior without punishment.

It is worth noting that these same strategies work with small groups of children as well. As you begin to address the misbehavior of the group, move to the group and call attention to the group's misbehavior. Sometimes this can involve speaking to one child or addressing the entire group. Then remind the group of the established expectations and solicit a commitment from the group to change their behavior.

Often, holding a conversation to clarify the desired behavior can help the child master that behavior. Setting a behavior goal with a child can formalize her decision to apply that behavior and use self-control.

Setting Behavior Goals

Not all children need the support of setting behavior goals or signing behavior contracts. However, some children do benefit from having their behavior formalized in this way. It is enough for some children to write a commitment down and sign their name. Other children need more reminders and support.

> Der mom
> I was itruting
> The clas mom
> I wot do It
> agin
> Love Kyla.

Formal Behavior Commitments

Before any behavior goal is set, sit down together with the child to discuss the problem. This might be done while other children are involved in a task, but it needs to be a private time between the two of you. Outside influences must be addressed so that the child understands that he or she is in charge of controlling the behavior. If the child shifts the

> I, _____ , promise to change
> my behavior. I will _____
>
> _____
>
> _____
>
> _____
>
> Signature: _____

cause of the misbehavior to someone or something else, then that must be addressed. For example, if the child says, "I could have done the right thing but Jason made me…" then Jason needs to be brought into the conversation. Asking, "Jason, can you agree to…so that Hunter can…?" keeps the responsibility for the behavior with Hunter.

Since it is not realistic to ask a young child to concentrate on more than one behavior at a time, focus the conversation on one misbehavior, helping the child agree to something that is attainable. After an agreement is reached, record it in some manner.

To formalize a commitment, ask the child to record the desired behavior and sign the commitment. This could be as simple as outlining the agreement in a written document, like, "I agree to…" Keep forms similar to the one on page 117 on hand. The child keeps this form in a place where it will remind him or her of the agreement. You should sign the form as well, attesting to what you are agreeing to do to help the situation.

At other times it is effective for you to discuss the behavior with the child, then the child can write a note to his family about the situation. You might simply say, "James, we have talked about how you need to keep your hands to yourself without touching other people. Now you are not doing what you agreed to do. Please get a piece of paper and write a note to your family about your behavior." Then James writes a note about his behavior, takes it home, has it signed, and returns the note to school the next day. Writing a note puts the responsibility for informing the family on the child. This is a small step toward accepting responsibility for behavior.

> Dir Mom
> I poosht Marshall I
> em sorey
> Grayson

Behavior Logs

To help a child focus on a behavior that needs to be changed, you and the child can jointly keep a Behavior Log about that behavior. This is especially effective when a child repeatedly hurts (physically or emotionally) or picks on other children. For example, when Charles was in kindergarten, he repeatedly called other children in the class "chicken head" or "meatloaf" and punched them. He had two older brothers who called him these names and wrestled with him in a friendly way. The other children in the class did not like to be called these names—to them it was as offensive as a dirty word. Charles did not understand that the children in the class did not like to be called these names or punched. He did not have any other strategies for making friends or being accepted as a part of the group.

After repeated conversations about name-calling and punching, Charles's teacher began to write down every time Charles broke the agreement about avoiding name-calling and punching. When Charles broke the agreement, the teacher asked him to get his Behavior Log (see sample at right) and she wrote down brief notes about the time and offense. At the end of the day, Charles and the teacher reviewed the day's behavior and jointly decided if Charles's behavior was "happy, straight, or sad face." Charles took the Behavior Log home for his parents to review and sign. The process was repeated over several weeks with the teacher noting how Charles was learning to use other strategies to make friends and gain acceptance. There was not immediate improvement, but over time his behavior did change.

Hold conferences with children about their behavior and use a variety of strategies to reinforce these conversations. Young children are not going to change their behavior overnight. It takes much work on the part of all concerned to see improvements in behavior.

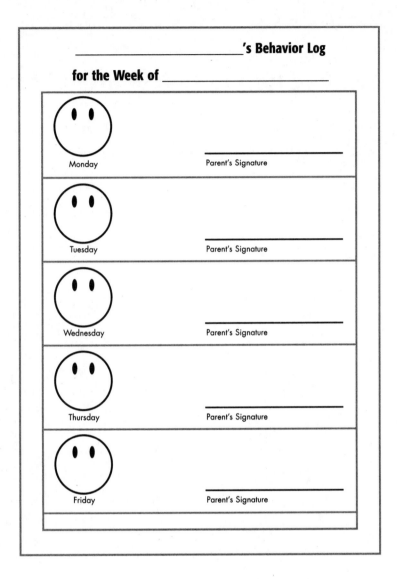

_____**'s Behavior Log**

for the Week of _____

Monday — Parent's Signature

Tuesday — Parent's Signature

Wednesday — Parent's Signature

Thursday — Parent's Signature

Friday — Parent's Signature

Looking for Improvement in Behavior

While it would be nice to think that a child's behavior will change after these procedures are implemented, that is not a realistic expectation. Many children need numerous conversations about improving behavior and numerous other interventions. The overarching goal is to improve the child's behavior one step at a time so the child learns to control his or her own behavior without constant adult supervision. Sometimes the results of the efforts are not observed until the next year or for an even longer period of time.

Students know that teachers care when improvement,
not perfection, is encouraged.
— *Jane Nelsen, Lynn Lott, and H. Stephen Glenn, 2000*

Comments
From a Kindergarten Teacher

Marcus was driving me crazy. It was only the second day of school, and already I was so frustrated that I wanted to cry. It didn't matter what I asked him to do. He was going to do the opposite. When we were singing, Marcus was sitting on the floor with his hands over his ears. When we were sitting quietly, listening to a story, Marcus was jumping up and down, singing at the top of his lungs. When we were having self-selected centers, Marcus demanded that I read a story. He ran all around the class. He pushed children who got in his way. It felt like Marcus was totally out of control.

I thought I had to bring Marcus's family into the situation. I called them and we decided to meet after school the next Friday. That afternoon I sat with Marcus and his mom, and described some of the behaviors I had observed that week. I managed to stay very calm and explain that I could not let Marcus continue to disturb the class the way he had that week. Then I pulled out a contract I had typed up the night before. It was simple. It just said, "Marcus promises to come to group meetings and be quiet so other children can hear." There were lots of other behaviors Marcus needed to change, but I chose the one that I wanted to work on first. I explained that I would walk over to Marcus before each group meeting and tell him what was about to happen. Then I would expect Marcus to walk to the meeting area and sit quietly right beside my chair. I asked Marcus if he could do that. He agreed, so we practiced several times, with Marcus's mother watching us. Then I suggested that she remind Marcus about our conversation each morning when she dropped him off at the school. There was not a miraculous change in Marcus's behavior that second week of school, but there were differences.

Over the next three months, Marcus, his mom, and I met every other Friday. We wrote and signed behavior contracts, and over time Marcus's behavior became more acceptable. Slowly, but surely.

We agree with Zemelman, Daniels, and Hyde's statement in their book, *Best Practice: New Standards for Teaching and Learning in America's Schools*:

> As classroom teachers ourselves, we are well aware of the luck of the draw and the year-to-year roulette of "good" and "bad" classes of students. Yet we believe that groups are mainly made, not inherited. There are specific, reliable ways for teachers to establish a productive classroom climate, and thus open the way to many promising innovations. (1998, p. 203)

When school personnel work together with families, improvement can be seen. We suggest reviewing children's behavior records and celebrating the small (or large) improvements each child is making. Focusing on the positive events is important in every guidance situation. Through this we can help children learn to be more self-reliant and self-controlled.

Summary

As the year continues, keep supporting children's appropriate behavior. Use class meetings to reinforce rules and routines, but keep in mind that some children need additional support. For these children, hold individual conversations about their behaviors; set behavior goals, creating behavior contracts when appropriate; and look for—and celebrate—small steps of improved behavior.

Final Words From Deborah

Some of you may be thinking, "This sounds good, but _____." There are all kinds of statements that might be used to fill in that blank. You may be thinking, "But I teach in a pretty rough inner-city school. That won't work in my school." You may believe that some young children could handle this kind of responsibility, but not your students.

The year I committed to having daily class meetings, to using one rule, "Be self-controlled," and to setting up routines for logistics and academics, I taught the most difficult group of kindergarten children that ever walked into my classroom. Included in that group of 23 students were:

- one boy who had been abandoned by his parents and was being raised by his 70-year-old grandparents. While he was in my class, he was kidnapped by his biological mother only to be abandoned again a few weeks later. He used scratching and biting to get his way.

- one girl whose father was in the state penitentiary for murder. She was a gentle girl most of the time, but she had sporadic outbursts that seemed to have no particular impetus.

- one boy who was prone to screaming bouts when he did not get his way. His screaming began with him repeating, "I hate you. I hate this school. I want to go home." His voice got louder and his words more angry as he went, and each episode would last anywhere from 15 to 45 minutes, with as many as three or four episodes a day.

- one girl who had been abused by her parents and was in the process of being adopted by relatives. She was timid to the nth degree. She would sob uncontrollably when asked to make a decision, anything from what she wanted to eat for lunch to which learning center she wanted to work in.

- one boy who had not been allowed inside his house during daylight hours since the time he was a toddler. Basically he had

grown up alone in his backyard with his dog and a box of dry cereal.
He took what he wanted and used any physical method necessary—
including hitting, kicking, and biting.

◆   one boy who was very bright cognitively, but did not have the
social skills needed to get along with his peers. He did things all the
time that caused other students to think he was weird, such as
sneaking around during quiet time to lick people's shoes.

If ever there was a year when I would not have given power to my students, this would
have been the year. These children were five years old and so many of them were coping with
serious life issues. But by the end of the year, I was absolutely convinced that class meetings,
guidelines, and routines were the better way of helping children develop. I saw more growth
in this group of children than in any other year that I had taught. My yearlong commitment
became a lifelong commitment.

Final Words From Charlotte

I began my career, as any fresh-out-of-school teacher does, thinking that I could handle anything that came my way. Then I was alone with the children and did not know what I was actually supposed to do. Oh sure, my mother was a teacher and I had grown up around her teacher friends, helping decorate her room at the beginning of every school year. And I made good grades in college and was successful with student teaching—but I still didn't have a clue about the best way for children to learn or how to make learning meaningful for them. I just did what it said to do in the teacher's manual.

Unfortunately, my teacher's manuals did not address the key issue of setting up classroom routines to help the class's day go smoothly. While I had the manuals to help me with the subject areas, I did not have a resource where I could learn how to successfully organize the classroom or the class's day. I could not figure out what went wrong when children had the least bit of independence. They went wild, doing things they would never do if I was standing over them. So I adopted a controlling, heavily teacher-directed method in my classroom.

Then I joined a group of teachers working to establish a new school in the district, one dedicated to helping children learn in real-world ways. It was through observing these colleagues and talking with them that I changed my thinking. I realized that establishing classroom routines and teaching children strategies for accepting responsibility benefited the children in multiple ways. I've also learned to see the "big picture." My job is to prepare the children to be competent citizens in the world, not just spout back facts. Instead of orchestrating every little move that every child has to make, I use phrases like "that's a decision you'll have to make," or "do the right thing" as I help and support the children as they learn to think, be self-reliant, and accept responsibility for their learning.

References

Aiex, Nola Kortner. "Bibliotherapy." *ERIC Digest*, ERIC Reproduction Service Document #ED357333, 1993.

Bickart, Toni S., Judy Jablon, and Diane Trister Dodge. *Building the Primary Classroom: A Complete Guide to Teaching and Learning*. Washington, D.C.: Teaching Strategies Inc., 1999.

Cameron, Caren, Betty Tate, Daphne MacNaughton, and Colleen Politano. *Recognition Without Rewards*. Manitoba, Canada: Peguis Publishers, 1997.

Charney, Ruth Sidney. *Teaching Children to Care*. Greenfield, MA: Northeast Foundation for Children, 1991.

Child Development Project. *Ways We Want Our Class to Be: Class Meetings That Build Commitment to Kindness and Learning*. Oakland, CA: Developmental Studies Center, 1996.

Clayton, Marlynn with Mary Beth Forton. *Classroom Spaces That Work*. Greenfield, MA: Northeast Foundation for Children, 2000.

Cunningham, Patricia, and Richard Allington. *Classrooms That Work: They Can All Read and Write*, 2nd ed. Boston: Addison-Wesley, 1998.

Dacey, Linda Schulman, and Rebeka Eston. *Growing Mathematical Ideas in Kindergarten*. Sausalito, CA: Math Solutions Publications, 1999.

Denton, Paula, and Roxann Kriete. *The First Six Weeks of School*. Greenfield, MA: Northeast Foundation for Children, 1999.

DeVries, Rheta, and Betty Zan. *Moral Classrooms, Moral Children: Creating a Constructivist Atmosphere in Early Education*. New York: Teachers College Press, 1994.

Dewey, John. *Experience and Education*. Carmichael, CA: Touchstone Books, 1938/1997.

Dewey, John. *The School and Society*. Chicago: University of Chicago Press, 1900/1990.

Diffily, Deborah, and Charlotte Sassman. *Project-Based Learning With Young Children.* Portsmouth, NH: Heinemann, 2002.

Graves, Donald. *Writing: Teachers and Children at Work.* Portsmouth, NH: Heinemann, 1983.

Kohn, Alfie. *Beyond Discipline: From Compliance to Community.* Alexandria, VA: Association for Supervision and Curriculum Development, 1996.

Kohn, Alfie. "Five Reasons to Stop Saying 'Good Job!'" *Young Children,* 56, no.5 (2001): 24–28.

Kohn, Alfie. *"The Risks of Rewards."* ERIC Digest, EDO-PS94-14, 1994.

Kohn, Alfie. *The Schools Our Children Deserve: Moving Beyond Traditional Classrooms and "Tougher Standards."* Boston: Houghton Mifflin, 1999.

Kriete, Roxann with Lynn Bechtel. *The Morning Meeting Book.* Greenfield, MA: Northeast Foundation for Children, 1999.

Landau, Barbara McEwan, and Paul Gathercoal. "Creating Peaceful Classrooms," *Phi Delta Kappan,* 81, no. 6, (2000): 450–454.

Nelsen, Jane, and H. Stephen Glenn. *Positive Discipline.* New York: Ballantine Books, 1996.

Nelsen, Jane, Lynn Lott, and H. Stephen Glenn. *Positive Discipline in the Classroom: Developing Mutual Respect, Cooperation, and Responsibility in Your Classroom* (rev. 3rd. ed.). New York: Prima Publishing, 2000.

Pardeck, John T. "Children's Literature and Child Abuse," *Child Welfare* 69, no. 1 (1990): 83–89.

Perlmutter, Jane, and Louise Burrell. *The First Weeks of School: Laying a Quality Foundation.* Portsmouth, NH: Heinemann, 2001.

Rich, Dorothy. *Megaskills: Building Children's Achievement for the Information Age*. Boston: Mariner Books, 1999.

Taberski, Sharon. *On Solid Ground*. Portsmouth, NH: Heinemann, 2000.

Zemelman, Steven, Harvey Daniels, and Arthur Hyde. *Best Practice: New Standards for Teaching and Learning in America's Schools*, 2nd ed. Portsmouth, NH: Heinemann, 1998.